Melville and Male Identity

Melville
and Male Identity

Charles J. Haberstroh, Jr.

Rutherford ● Madison ● Teaneck
Fairleigh Dickinson University Press
London and Toronto ● Associated University Presses

©1980 by Associated University Presses, Inc.

Associated University Presses, Inc.
Cranbury, New Jersey 08512

Associated University Presses
Magdalen House
136-148 Tooley Street
London SE1 2TT, England

Associated University Presses
Toronto M5E 1A7, Canada

Library of Congress Cataloging in Publication Data

Haberstroh, Charles
Melville and male identity.

Bibliography: p.
1. Melville, Herman, 1819-1891. 2. Melville,
Herman, 1819-1891--Biography--Character.
3. Masculinity (Psychology) 4. Novelists, American
--19th century--Biography. I. Title.
PS2386.H3   813'.3   78-75178
ISBN 0-8386-2321-2

Printed in the United States of America

KM
3-17-82

To Pat, Ethan, and Karintha

Contents

Acknowledgments

I would like most especially to thank Hennig Cohen, who remained throughout the project a sympathetic and shrewd critic, and whose support and suggestions at a difficult juncture in the manuscript's progress helped me to take fresh directions.

Also, I am grateful for permission to quote from the following works: *Melville,* by Edwin H. Miller. Copyright ©1975, with permission of George H. Braziller, Inc.; *Herman Melville: Cycle and Epicycle,* by Eleanor Melville Metcalf. Copyright ©1953, with permission of Harvard University Press; *The Letters of Herman Melville,* edited by Merrell R. Davis and William H. Gilman. Copyright ©1960, with permission of Yale University Press; *The Fine Hammered Steel of Herman Melville,* by Milton Stern. Copyright ©1957, with permission of the University of Illinois Press; *The Gansevoorts of Albany,* by Alice P. Kenney. Copyright ©1969, with permission of Syracuse University Press; *Herman Melville: A Biography,* by Leon Howard. Copyright ©1951, with permission of the University of California Press; "Melville, Marriage, and *Mardi,*" by Charles J. Haberstroh, Jr. Copyright ©1977, with permission of *Studies in the Novel,* North Texas State University; "*Redburn:* The Psychological Pattern," by Charles J. Haberstroh, Jr. Copyright ©1974, with permission of *Studies in American Fiction,* Northeastern University; *Melville's Early*

Life and Redburn, by William H. Gilman. Copyright ©1951, with permission of the estate of William H. Gilman; *Billy Budd,* edited by Harrison Hayford and Merton M. Sealts, Jr. Copyright ©1962, with permission of the University of Chicago Press. I have relied wherever possible on the Northwestern-Newberry edition of Melville's works, edited by Harrison Hayford, Hershel Parker, and G. Thomas Tanselle, and published by Northwestern University Press and the Newberry Library.

Lastly, I would like to thank Mary Elizabeth Boyle for her valuable assistance in the preparation of the manuscript.

Melville and Male Identity

1

Melville and His Family

WHEN Ishmael asks, toward the end of *Moby-Dick,* "Where is the foundling's father hidden?" (p. 406),[1] he presumes that if one could find this lost father, one could also discover "the final harbor," the "rapt ether . . . of which the weariest will never weary" (p. 406). The orphan's discovery of a lost parent would constitute an entry into a tireless and timeless world of golden peace: the final escape, the final freedom from doubt, the final and safe pillow for the head of the troubled child. No more need he wake up to the "nameless, unimaginable, silent form or phantom" (p. 33) that can terrorize the night. Rather, he will hear what Melville later called in "The Enviable Isles" "a song to lull all sorrow and all glee,"[2] a soft suspension of the need to think, or hope, or fear. Past and future, memory and desire will dissolve into an eternally placid present: a bay from which one hears the beating of the sea waves, but where the currents of the sea have no authority. One floats, rests, and watches the sun spread light across the surrounding landscape, while, only dimly perceived through a haze of forgetfulness, the waves grind and toss themselves at some gentle shore:

"Dimpling in dream—unconscious slumberers mere,/While billows endless round the beaches die."[3] At sea, of course, Ishmael must fight the daily changes of wind and current, must be skilled in the constant manipulation of ship's gear, must be wary, alert, strong, unsentimental, and able to accept ambiguity. But he yearns to know when he can rest; an orphan, he feels most comfortable in the paternal presence of Queequeg, that prince among chiefs who has adopted the wandering Ishmael as his own. Ishmael urges his readers to be faithful not to a life amid the welter of the sea, but to hug close to the "insular Tahiti" (p. 236) that each of them privately possesses, and that he experiences when he and Queequeg share the intimate isolation of the Spouter Inn. There, sheltered by the strength and self-possession of his friend, Ishmael feels his soul and mind become healed. While the life of a sailor has its excitements and joys, it also has too many dangers to both body and spirit. The ultimate good is a world that is the antithesis of the sea: a place of green fields and fatherly presences.

This is true not only for Ishmael but also for the author who glooms out from behind his experiences. Melville himself associated the figure of the father with a world of peace and contentment, the world, in fact, of his own childhood in New York during the 1820s. As the son of Allan Melville, a man whose home was a comfortable mixture of money, good taste, and respectable connections, and who had "acquired an international reputation for trustworthiness,"[4] Herman lived with seeming impunity away from the shocks and recognitions about life that others less fortunate (like the starving children Melville saw in Liverpool later on) had to endure. Because of the status of his father and the genteel power that status embodied, Herman grew to expect an endless chain of tranquil intensities amid the accoutrements of an unshakably middle-class life. Certainly he was not prepared for any sounds but the settling hum of afternoons among the Melville livingroom's portfolios and foreign furniture. Unfortunately, however, the chain was broken for Herman on two occasions—his father's commercial failure in New York in 1830, and then his maniacal death two years later in Albany. Into Melville's life for the first time intruded the experience of serious loss, the inevitably disappointing cycle of living. From his father's room, in his father's death cries, he heard the prefigurement of the gull's scream that cuts the heart in half, and felt then, long before going to sea, the grey music of storm swells. So Melville, in becoming a sailor at age nineteen, only followed what was already inevitable for him, the destiny that had been his before he ever knew that a shroud could be anything but burial garments. By the age of thirteen he had seen those "flotillas of spectre-boats" he would write about later in *Pierre*[5]; and the vision seemed to cancel forever the dear dreams of safety that had cradled his childhood.

Melville's emotional life was permanently skewed by this new vision, and by the loss of status the family underwent because of Allan Melville's failure and death. It had been, after all, such a surprise. And, as Herman grew up—indeed, for as long as he lived—his father's misfortune must have seemed to him to have been the final pressure that tipped the scale against his own future, pushing him, permanently and rudderlessly, into the world's hazardous currents. His continual use of homeless sailor-narrators in his fiction indicates an early sense of the inevitability of his own loneliness and defeat, of the ultimate victory of some unseen force that singled certain families out for pursuit. Herman discovered that he was only part of a tragic plan for the Melvilles projected from the impersonal ruminations of a deity like the one in *Moby-Dick* who self-sufficiently inhabited the "heartless voids and immensities" (p. 169) of his own eternal life, and cared nothing for those whose temporal lives he so arbitrarily and cruelly designed. There was no final escape from the stroke of the axe. "A born thrall to the last, . . . [man] still remains a slave unto Oro [God]."[6]

The Gansevoorts, his mother's people, might constellate in Dutch solidity around their upstate New York patrimonies, the products of a happier fate; but the Melville patriarchs seemed doomed to be shoved about until circumstances finally jostled them to death. Herman had an object lesson in this not only from the tragic history of his father, but also from the condition of his father's older brother, Thomas. Once a wealthy man in France, he was, by the time young Herman became familiar with him, painfully poor and living with his numerous children on a Massachusetts farm, which, though handsomely designated "Broadhall," barely provided him with food and clothing. Herman, who spent almost a year on the farm in 1834, remembered him "by the late October fire, . . . gazing into the embers, his face plainly expressing to a sympathetic observer that his heart . . . carried him far away over the ocean to the gay Boulevards [of Paris]."[7] Thomas, like his brother, Allan, had wound up a far cry from his affluent and prominent father, Thomas Melville, Sr., who in Herman's memory remained a man with a "broad-breasted vest, coming bravely down over the hips, and furnished with two strong-boxes of pockets to keep guineas in."[8] Nor were Allan Melville's oldest sons ever able to fill the family pockets again. Three years after Herman's stay with his Uncle Thomas, Gansevoort, Herman's older brother, was bankrupt at the ripe old age of twenty-two. It had been Gansevoort who had always seemed most eminently ready to pick up his father's slack; he was the favorite son, the one always considered talented. But his attempt to restore the family fortunes through the fur business, while briefly successful, ended in 1837 as his father's own mercantile career in New York had in 1830. As time went on Gansevoort drifted into law, then politics, at which his party considered him brilliant but undependable, and then into a minor consular post in England where, from all evidence, he died in (and from) the same sorts of mental turmoil his father had. Herman himself, when it came time for him to bear some significant responsibility for the family, could only go from being an unsuccessful author, to being an unsuccessful lecturer, to being an anonymous customs collector. Then, in 1867 at home, Herman's oldest son, Malcolm, shot himself through the head under unexplained circumstanes. And in 1886, his only other son, Stanwix, died of tuberculosis in San Francisco, never having been anything but an itinerant and luckless drifter. Each crop of Melville sons seemed more blighted and vulnerable than the next. It is signficant that Herman's mother, Maria Gansevoort Melville, spent the last part of her life in Gansevoort, New York, retreating back symbolically, perhaps, into the shelter of a place that bore the maiden name she had relinquished in marrying Allan Melville. The Gansevoort patronymic was history; it was respectability; it was money. The Melville name had become only a sound with no meaning or honor.

While Herman may have often felt like a useless spectator at his family's (and his own) decline, he was also acutely sensitive to the pressures from both sides of his ancestry for male aggressiveness and worldly success. He may have felt like an abandoned and impotent child whose greatest wish was to repose, once again, in the safe bosom of some father's seeming strength, but he was also a man in a family where men aspired to wealth and position. Even his father, regardless of his failures, was committed to this view of masculine responsibility, and presented to the young and impressionable Herman a constant reminder of the importance of conspicuous achievement. The son of a prosperous Boston merchant and major in the Revolutionary War, Allan Melville could be "traced . . . back in direct lineal descent to Sir Richard de Melville, Knight in the reign of Alexander the 3rd in the year 1268."[9] In fact, the Melvilles were "of a royal line in both sides of the House,"[10] something that Allan Melville felt "should produce a . . . spirit of emulation in their descendants to the remotest posterity."[11] It certainly produced that spirit in him, and bathed his 1818 trip to the ancestral lands in

Scotland in a glorious nostalgia. But he was not one for living on nostalgia or past glory. As the product of family piety and steadiness, coupled with a good education, the grand tour, twenty months in Paris, and a number of years of varying (but respectable) fortunes as an importer in Boston and Albany, he began, in 1818, the New York importing business that over the next twelve years was to bring him at least the appearance of considerable prosperity. He was traveled, both in Europe and America; his social contacts were extensive and certainly of the best sort; he was well-read, fluent in French, moderate in religion, concerned for the welfare of his family, and a collector of foreign books and *objets d'art*. Over the period from 1818 to 1830, he marked his rise in the commercial firmament in New York by moves to more and more pleasant homes, culminating in the 1828 move to a house at 675 Broadway.

> The house, though narrow, had a center staircase, numerous bedrooms, some with fireplaces and marble mantelpieces, and an upstairs sitting room "with a handsome Cornish round it." The deep yard behind held "a fine Garden prettily laid out with fruit trees shrubbery bulbous roots &c fine Grass plot and woodhouse," and with a vacant lot on one side there was a "delightful opening and pure air" for boyish sports.[12]

One can certainly agree with William Gilman that "the two and a half years Herman spent in these surroundings were probably the happiest of his life";[13] and in 1828, Allan Melville seemed the invulnerable guardian of that domestic world, the biggest sun on Herman's horizon.

Therefore, even if Herman were later to come to know that in truth his father's prosperity had often been jury-rigged on overextended credit, still the thrust of his father's ambitions, that desire to constantly rise in the world's eyes, inevitably served as a model for young Herman of what was expected of a Melville male. In addition, from his father in particular, but reinforced by the style of his uncle Thomas' early life, there was a strain of cultured cosmopolitanism that was part of his inherited social consciousness—his father and his uncle, unlike the Gansevoorts on his mother's side, had been places. Their careers had attempted to join commercial aspiration to a romantic internationalism. Allan "was very different from Albany boys like [Maria Gansevoort's] brothers. Herman [Gansevoort's] mind was always on his mills, L.H.'s on his ledgers, Peter's on his lawbooks, but [Allan] Melville had learned the manners of a gentleman in the refining atmosphere of Paris. Nine years older than Maria, distinguished and attractive, he liked to read and exercise his imagination fashioning elegant compliments and delicate attentions."[14] It was perhaps this strain in both Allan's and Thomas' personalities that finally ruined them, which did not allow them so total a concentration on matters of commerce as the Gansevoorts always showed, who were traditionally uninterested in literature or the arts. And whether the memories of Allan's playing the gentleman were, in their turn, a blessing or a curse for the formation of his own sons' and grandsons' personalities is an open question. Gansevoort, for example, turned out to be something of a fop, and his political career shows him a good bit more devoted to party rhetoric than practical politics. Melville's own impractical literary career is surely in part a by-blow of remembrances of Allan Melville's "style." Even Malcolm Melville's joy in strutting about in his military uniform, carrying prominently the gun that finally killed him, may have been the last grimly ironical flourish of the spirit of Allan Melville. But whatever its long-term effects, in Allan Melville's house Herman must have come to feel that, in addition to social and financial achievment, there was also the necessity for a Melville male to establish some sort of genteel cosmopolitan identity, something to give one's wealth and status broader scope for activity than Albany or New York.

While Albany may not have been the world, however, the

pressures toward success and male assertiveness among his
mother's family were even more intense than what he saw in
his father, largely because of the dynastic capitalism of the
upstate Dutch.

> . . . . Dutch merchants handed over their valuable but in-
> tangible network of credit and commercial contacts intact
> to their sons. The roster of patrician families in Dutch
> cities and in Albany, therefore, remained stable for genera-
> tions while in English cities and English colonial towns the
> turnover of families in the merchant oligarchy was rapid.[15]

The Gansevoorts were one of the oldest patrician merchant
families in Albany, and Herman bore the name of three of
their most important members: Harmen Gansevoort
(1635-1710), the original settler of the family, and instigator
of its upward mobility; Harme Gansevoort (1712-1801),
Melville's great-grandfather, who first securely established
the family in the Albany Dutch patriciate; and Herman
Gansevoort (1779-1862), Melville's uncle, a more than wor-
thy, and wealthy, successor to his share of Harmen and
Harme's patrimony.

> [Herman Gansevoort] was by far the largest taxpayer in the
> township; in the first years of the century, the Gansevoorts
> were sometimes called upon to pay $100 in taxes and to
> contribute 100 days of labor on the roads. In 1827 Herman
> was assessed for about 10 per cent of the town's total taxes
> and the next highest taxpayer, the Fort Miller Bridge Com-
> pany, paid only a third as much as he.[16]

Melville was for his entire life also very much in awe of the
one Gansevoort who dominated the whole family's attention:
General Peter Gansevoort, Melville's grandfather, whose
defense of Fort Stanwix during the Revolution remained
always a source of family pride, and whose presence hovered
heroically in the back of both the Melville and Gansevoort
family consciousnesses as an emblem of not only admirable

wealth, but of patriotic duty "to the last extremity"[17]—a kind of Dutch Lord Nelson. Allan Melville quite proudly wore the General's ring and Herman named his younger son Stanwix after the General's historic holding-action, just as he had named his older son Malcolm in tribute to his father's Scottish ancestry. As late as 1870, Herman demonstrated the continuing hold the General's image had on his mind when he visited the Gansevoort Hotel in New York, to see if anyone were familiar with the family name.

> I bought a paper of tobacco by way of introducing myself: then I said to the person who served me: "Can you tell me what this word 'Gansevoort' means? . . . ." Thereupon a solemn gentleman at a remote table spoke up: "Sir," said he, putting down his newspaper, "this hotel and the street of the same name are called after a very rich family who in old times owned a great deal of property hereabouts." The dense ignorance of this solemn gentleman,—his knowing nothing of the hero of Fort Stanwix, aroused such an indignation in my breast, that, disdaining to enlighten his benighted soul, I left the place without further colloquy . . . .[18]

"Herman's social background [on the Gansevoort side] was unimpeachable, and he was undoubtedly aware of the distinction it furnished,"[19] as well as the obligations it entailed: financial success, family loyalty, and devotion to duty. The Gansevoorts were ever-vigilant for "opportunities for promoting the advantage of their families and protecting the privileges of their community."[20]

The painful thing for Melville, enmeshed in this family matrix of powerful status models, was that while he certainly felt some necessity of discharging his inherited male responsibilities, he was at the same time resentful over that necessity, and desirous of being freed forever from it. For example, when he married in 1847, and so chose to take upon himself the roles of husband and provider, it is clear that this assumption of responsibility was only a source of anxiety for him. In particular, Melville always conspicuously praised the bachelor life and denigrated marriage, a cynicism about domestic institutions that seems traceable in large part to powerful uncertainties about his ability, or even desire, to be head of a household. These uncertainties may also be the causes behind his often hostile attitudes toward women.

> His females are dolls like Fayaway in *Typee* or viragoes like Mrs. Glendinning in *Pierre,* implausible and unreal as characters, although they threaten the heroes by arousing fears surrounding either marriage and domestication or castration. Love, romantic or tragic, Melville could not handle except parodistically.[21]

Women were the chief lure toward the commitments to the masculine traditions of the Melville and Gansevoort clans that he did not believe he could live up to. By succumbing to the temptation to marry and have a family, Melville seems to have felt both socially and sexually coerced into a situation where he could only imagine his inadequacies as dominating, and where, in fact, they did more often than not (he *was,* as it turned out, an ineffectual breadwinner). It is not surprising, then, that he would resent women, whom he felt in good part to be the cause of his impossible situation. At the same time, women represented, for an individual like Melville who persistently conceived of himself as deserted by his father, sources of crucial maternal support, and ultimately even ways of putting him in touch, through family connections, with surrogate fathers for the desperate orphan child at the center of his psyche. Even this, however, could not produce tranquility, because part of Melville hated that child, was embarrassed by his presence, and resented his weakness and naiveté. Indeed, in *Pierre,* Melville would try to murder the child and so destroy his own attachment to his dream of restoring somehow for himself his lost, idyllic boyhood.

The pattern of reliance on women, and through them, on the protection of males more powerful and affluent than

Melville himself could ever become, started after the failure of Gansevoort's fur business, when the family drew its financial support mainly from his Uncle Peter Gansevoort, the most patrician of Maria Melville's patrician brothers. Then, when Herman married Elizabeth Shaw—a marriage commentators have always suspected was especially attractive to Melville because of the paternal presence of Lizzie's father, Judge Lemuel Shaw—he took his mother (and even his four sisters) to live with him, and began also what became a lifelong habit of accepting aid from his new father-in-law. It was Judge Shaw, for instance, who paid Herman's share of his first home at 103 Fourth Avenue in New York. It was also Judge Shaw who bought Arrowhead for Herman and Lizzie in 1850, and then in 1860 accepted the deed to the property in order to cancel all of Melville's debts to him, only to turn back around and convey the deed to Lizzie in an act of characteristic generosity toward his daughter and her impecunious husband. Even after Lemuel Shaw's death and well into Melville's old age, it was Shaw money that helped keep Melville afloat, just as Queequeg's coffin keeps the orphan Ishmael from sinking. One of the principal things that allowed for the tranquility of Melville's last years was the fact that when the Judge's son, Lemuel, Jr., died in 1884, the Melville children each received $2,000 from the Judge's estate, and Elizabeth received over $33,000.

At times, however, the very helpfulness with which people responded to Melville became an unpleasant reminder for him of his unmanly dependency. One such instance occurred in 1876-1877 with Catherine Gansevoort Lansing, his Uncle Peter Gansevoort's daughter. In 1875 Uncle Peter had advanced Herman $1200 for *Clarel's* publication; but when, after Peter's death, the publication costs turned out to be more than the advance, Catherine Lansing, assuming as the family always did that Melville would not have the necessary cash, pressed upon him the sum of $100. Melville did not want to take it, and one of his letters to her at this time shows Melville's discomfort over his inability to establish himself in any dynamic way in the eyes of his own family.

> As it turned out, the 1200 covered the printing expenses, with a fraction to spare. But the supplementary charges—not long ago brought to my attention—against the account of the book—advertisting &c, and customary copies distributed for advertising purposes—will make a difference with me in any receipts to come, of about one hundred dollars.
>
> Whether this comes within the scope of Uncle Peter's design or not, I do not venture to determine. But enough.—
>
> Lizzie got your note yesterday. I thank you again for your repeated invitation to come up & spend some Sunday with you. I should be most happy so to do if practicable.
>
> Lizzie and Fanny (Fanny the Little) are busily completing their arrangements for the White Mountain campaign.—Lizzie and I went to see Tom at the island . . . .[22]

Tactfully Melville changes the subject of the letter to domestic inanities because the real matter of the letter is not the money, or the White Mountains, but rather the fact that Melville, age fifty-six, has spent so long taking financial help from others that the role of public charge has become permanently associated with him, regardless of whether he actually needs help or not. And so Melville, before he might choke on the bitter image of himself that the letter he must write conjures up, leaps into the confidential cousin role that obscures that image (after all, the letter tries to say, between two cousins who understand one another so well, what could be embarrassing?). When Catherine actually sent him the money, he gave her one hundred dollar draft, in a very self-conscious gesture, to the New York Society for the Relief of the Ruptured and Crippled. Unfortunately, the bottomlessly goodhearted Catherine sent him another check (she only wished to help him, and never appreciated the abiding edge of irony and self-hatred that made him donate the first money to charity). Herman, however, stuck to his guns and returned the check. In part this was, as Leon Howard indicates, perhaps "only because he had received $500 from the estate of his Uncle Peter,"[23]; but surely it was also, by Melville's lights, a genuine gesture toward his own past acquiescences. Every gift he had taken had become a part of the record of his failure as a breadwinner, the domestic failure he had probably always known he would be, and that his marriage had forced him into constantly displaying. None of the people who aided Melville ever sought to humble him; but his position as sometime charity case could not help but give his life a special tinge of desperation and sadness: the memory of a hope of a childhood Eden no longer possible, compounded by the necessary assumption of adult male responsibilities he could never adequately bear.

There was, however, one way he might partially resolve his emotional conflicts and grasp at the best of both worlds: a way to play out the role of strong, assertive male, while remaining passive and dependent in his practical relations with his family and the world. In 1846, he began taking that way by publishing *Typee*. Through authorship, Melville might develop a public identity that made him more, somehow, than just another anonymous ex-sailor boy, or the unsuccessful son of a failed father. For instance, the pages of *Typee*, dominated by Melville 's autobiographical *persona*, Tommo, created a personal public history for its author—not as grand, perhaps, as that of his grandfather, the General, nor of his father or Uncle Thomas in their youthful heydays, but at least an affirmation that he had done interesting and colorful things that others only dream about. As it turned out, both *Typee* and *Omoo* also showed Melville's inability, from the outset, to have his narrators live up to the image he wanted to give of himself; but, at least on the surface, Melville could have Tommo demonstrate the possession of those masculine traits he had come to associate with the two families of which he was indelibly a product. Tommo is presented as being knowledgeable, resourceful, sensible, and dependable. The last item, especially, had great importance for Melville. He was enormously concerned over claims that his narrative was not true, concerned enough to go so far as to include in the revised edition "The Story of Toby" as a sequel to prove the accuracy of his account. Besides the danger of falling sales if people came to believe the novel were only a romance rather than a true adventure, there seem to be two crucial psychological reasons for Melville's concern. Doubt about the veracity of the book would mean suspicions that the narrator was simply a fabrication, and so bore little or no real relation to the author. This would effectually deny Melville's bid for male identity through his work, and leave him, in terms of his public presence, exactly where he had been before picking up his pen. Melville wanted *himself,* not "Tommo," to be known as the man who had lived among cannibals. Also, true and accurate accountings were considered an essential virtue among Dutch merchants, and were surely part of the Gansevoort code of honor.

> When a Man happens to break in *Holland,* they say of him that *he has not kept true Accompts.* This Phrase, perhaps, amongst us would appear a soft or humorous way of speaking, but with that exact Nation it bears the highest Reproach; for a Man to be mistaken in the Calculation of His Expence, in his Ability to answer future Demands, or to be impertinently sanguine in putting his Credit to too great Adventure, are all Instances of as much Infamy, as with gayer Nations to be failing in Courage or common Honesty.[24]

As with commerce, so with one's other relations. The man who set no store by accuracy, who did not get his facts right, or misrepresented himself or his capacities, had little honor, and was not to be trusted. Herman, in *Typee,* had represented himself and his experiences in a particular light, a light that then had to be defended if he were to keep any face not only before the world at large, but before his own aunts, and uncles, and cousins.

The problem for Melville's career as it went on, however, was that he failed to maintain this credibility with his audience. Too regularly, what dominated Melville's work was the personality of the abandoned child rather than the responsible adult: bitter and self-absorbed, imagining itself hopelessly alone and adrift, it turned inward. "I talk all about myself, and this is selfishness and egotism. Granted. But how help it?"[25] His work only took on full importance for him when it could explore the complicated geography of his own idiosyncratic literary ideas rather than the external societies of Nukuheva, Tahiti, Liverpool, or a man-of-war. At the same time, he was still bitter over the fact that in following this imperative he had lost any chance of cultivating the public significance he had originally set out to win, and which he always craved. "Though I wrote the Gospels in this century, I should die in the gutter."[26] Part of Melville, after all, had to believe his talents as a writer could bring him money and recognition, if he did not weaken or get lazy. He imagined writing to be his sword, symbol of masculine potency, like the silver-hilted one of General Gansevoort that his family treasured.

Yet . . . are we scabbards to our souls. And the drawn soul of genius is more glittering than the drawn cimeter of Saladin. But how many let their steel sleep, till it eat up the scabbard itself, and both corrode to rust-chips. Saw you ever the hillocks of old Spanish anchors, and anchor-stocks of ancient galleons, at the bottom of Callao Bay? The world is full of old Tower armories, and dilapidated Venetian arsenals, and rusty old rapiers. But true warriors polish their good blades by the bright beams of the morning; and gird them on to their brave sirloins; and watch for

rust spots as for foes; and by many stout thrusts and stoc-
cadoes keep their metal lustrous and keen, as the spears of
the Northern Lights charging over Greenland.[27]

But while Melville used his blade, in books like *Typee* and
Omoo, or *Redburn* and *White-Jacket,* to serve up the meat of
that recognizable universe that had nourished the fame of his
ancestors, he also too easily became a knight-errant in a
chaotic interior landscape of abstractions, ambiguities, and
ontological phantoms. The voice that had seemed to halloo
so vigorously to his readers from the yards in *Typee* came to
sound often to his audience like some form of irrelevant gib-
berish. This was what, for example, so befuddled the readers
of *Moby-Dick.* Leading them on with the pretext of an exciting whaling cruise, Melville spends enormous amounts of
time in complicated intellection, presenting a disorienting
topography of language and idea where he is always looking
past the real objects and people aboard the Pequod to their
reflections in the altering mirror of his own romantic sen-
sibility. He had shown this tendency, indeed, already in *Mardi,* two years before *Moby-Dick,* where, giving only the most
cursory nod at a framework of identifiable reality for his
story, he had gone on to create a world not of real continents,
but of categories of experience, where the various islands and
characters became allegorical renderings of conditions of
consciousness. Even Elizabeth referred to the "fogs"[28] of
Mardi's difficult meanderings. In doing so, she voiced a concern over her husband's obscurantism that would become a
constant criticism of his work by other readers, and that
would, with the publication of *The Confidence-Man* in
1857,finally isolate him completely from the literary life of
his day.

Melville's personality in his works, therefore, tended to
confuse, annoy, and exasperate readers, as indeed it often did
himself. Battered by winds of conflicting emotion they could
not tack before, his writings gradually foundered. There was

no way in his fiction for him to clutch at any resolution of the ambivalences that riddled it, ambivalences caused by the tension between his hopeless and introverted sense of himself as a lost boy, and his desire to fulfill the extroverted traditions of male status, success, and assertiveness with which he grew up. As he complained to Hawthorne, "What I feel most moved to write, that is banned,—it will not pay. Yet, altogether, write the *other* way I cannot. So the product is a final hash, and all my books are botches."[29] From the point of view of Melville's desire to integrate his personality, he was substantially correct.

Notes

1. Harrison Hayford and Hershel Parker, eds., *Moby-Dick* (New York: W. W. Norton and Co., 1967).

2. Herman Melville, *John Marr and Other Sailors* (New York: De Vinne Press, 1888), p. 97.

3. Ibid.

4. William H. Gilman, *Melville's Early Life and Redburn* (New York: New York University Press, 1951), p. 7.

5. Harrison Hayford, Hershel Parker, and G. Thomas Tanselle, eds., *Pierre* (Evanston and Chicago: Northwestern University Press and the Newberry Library, 1971), p. 49.

6. Harrison Hayford, Hershel Parker, and G. Thomas Tanselle, eds., *Mardi* (Evanston and Chicago: Northwestern University Press and the Newberry Library, 1970), p. 528.

7. Gilman, p. 67.

8. Edwin Miller, *Melville* (New York: George Braziller, 1975), p. 58.

9. Gilman, p. 12.

10. Ibid.

11. Ibid., p. 13.

12. Ibid., p. 33.

13. Ibid.

14. Alice P. Kenney, *The Gansevoorts of Albany* (Syracuse: Syracuse University Press, 1969), p. 174.

15. Ibid., p. 22.

16. Ibid., pp. 149-150.

17. Ibid., p. 103

18. Letter of 5 May 1870, in Merrell R. Davis and William H. Gilman, eds., *The Letters of Herman Melville* (New Haven: Yale University Press, 1960), p. 235.

19. Gilman, p. 48.

20. Kenney, p. 78.

21. Miller, p. 117.

22. Letter of 25 July 1876, in Davis and Gilman, p. 246.

23. Leon Howard, *Herman Melville* (Berkeley: University of California Press, 1951), p. 311.
24. Kenney, p. 188.
25. Letter of 1 June 1851, in Davis and Gilman, p. 129.
26. Ibid.
27. *Mardi,* p. 104.
28. Eleanor Melville Metcalf, *Herman Melville: Cycle and Epicycle* (Cambridge: Harvard University Press, 1953), p. 61.
29. Letter of 1 June 1851, in Davis and Gilman, p. 128.

2

Typee and *Omoo*

WHATEVER heroic adventures Tommo's imagination charts for him at the beginning of *Typee,* he winds up using the Typee Valley finally as a place to hide out from his own insecurities. The exotic facts of Polynesian life, along with the geniality of Tommo's recounting of them, were enough to mask Tommo's weakness from Melville's readers and insure the book's success. But the assertive *persona* Melville wanted to develop in order to carry on in some way for himself the Melville-Gansevoort expectations of male behavior began to demonstrate, after a short time into his Polynesian narrative, a penchant for passivity and dependence. Granted, there is a flourish of spectactular activity in the first nine chapters, as Tommo and Toby indomitably press ever onward into Nukuheva, through suffocating canefields, narrow gorges, like "Belzoni, worming himself through the subterranean passages of the Egyptian catacombs" (p. 59),[1] and up and down perilous ravines—all in pursuit of the great expectations Tommo felt awaited them.

The Marquesas! What strange visions of outlandish things does the very name spirit up! Naked houris—cannibal banquets—groves of cocoa-nut—coral reefs—tatooed chiefs—and bamboo temples; sunny valleys planted with bread-fruit-trees—carved canoes dancing on the flashing blue waters—savage woodlands guarded by horrible idols—*heathenish rites and human sacrifices.* [P. 5]

Still, Typee once found does not become a ground on which Tommo exercises some dynamic physical or intellectual energy. Rather, it is a place tht easily coerces him into lying about in splendor, amid unfailing abundance, where his ineffectual self can be constantly ministered to by those he considers noblemen of nature, and whose cannibalism he even tries to rationalize away. Under the aegis of the imposing and benevolent Mehevi, the valley's most powerful chief, and snuggled in the bosom of a surrogate savage family composed of Tinor, Fayaway, Kory-Kory, and the fatherly old Marheyo, he substitutes comfort and passivity for his original adventurous intentions. There are always perfectly acceptable narrative reasons for this failure of assertiveness, but one suspects, knowing Melville, that the ultimate reason lies in Melville's own sense of inadequacy and the temptation to allow his narrator to fall into the role of dependent child in hopes of gaining support for him from individuals who would serve Melville's need to fictionally restore some of the security of his own childhood.

Actually, Tommo begins to lose his forcefulness by chapter 8, even before he and his companion reach the valley. He comes to rely on Toby, whose "fearless confidence . . . was contagious" (p. 58), to carry him psychologically across the final obstacles to their descent into the valley, just as later he comes to rely on Kory-Kory to carry him physically about the valley because of the incapacitating wound in his leg. The chance wound, in fact, provides a very convenient justification not only for Tommo's continued reliance on Toby (it can be left up to Toby to take any initiatives to get them out of the valley), but, more significantly, for his remaining a long-term guest of the Typees. With his wound as an explanation, there is no reason to feel guilt about his passivity, because who could criticize a disabled individual for playing a wait-and-see game, and reclining in the lap of the valley's ostensible hospitality. Any possible guilt feelings are only further lessened when Toby, who opposes what he considers Tommo's too benevolent interpretation of the Typees' motives, goes off to seek help and does not return. It is initially frightening to Tommo, because he wonders what, really, he has gotten himself into; but it seems finally to be what he always secretly wanted, what any child might secretly want: to be the pampered center of attention of his elders. "[N]ow that [Toby] was gone, the natives multiplied their acts of kindness and attention towards myself, treating me with a degree of deference which could hardly have been surpassed had I been some celestial visitant" (p. 109). And there is no chance that his inactive style of life will ever be censured by the natives, because it is, in fact, the style they all lead, physically incapacitated or not. Thus, Tommo is free to make of the valley whatever he wishes.

> . . . I gave myself up to the passing hour, and if ever disagreeable thoughts arose in my mind, I drove them away. When I looked around the verdant recess in which I was buried, and gazed up to the summits of the lofty eminence that hemmed me in, I was well disposed to think that I was in the "Happy Valley," and that beyond those heights there was nought but a world of care and anxiety. [P. 124]

His imagination can comfortably convert tomb to womb, and prison to "Happy Valley" of tranquil security.

This imagination is given fertile fields to play in. The actualities of Typee life, as they unfold for Tommo, seem to create just the sort of place for the lost and disappointed side of Melville to take up residence. In particular, Tommo focuses his attention on the patterns of family life and economics in the valley, aspects of the Typee culture important for Melville because together they create a psychological situation that eliminates most of the potential familial pressures Melville always felt trapped within. Tommo notes that "the natives appeared to form one household, whose members were bound together by the ties of strong affection" (p. 204). The natives practice polyandry, a woman usually forming a household with two men.

> The girls are first wooed and won, at a very tender age, by some stripling in the household in which they reside. This, however, is a mere frolic of the affections, and no formal engagement is contracted. By the time this first love has a little subsided, a second suitor presents himself, of graver years, and carries both boy and girl away to his own habitation. This disinterested and generous-hearted fellow now weds the young couple—marrying damsel and lover at the same time—and all three thenceforth live together as harmoniously as so many turtles. [P. 191]

It is significant that this system openly institutionalizes that relationship between husbands, wives, and third male parties that Melville later covertly sought to establish in his own marriage to Elizabeth Shaw, and his reliance on his father-in-law.

As a result of the Typee method of forming families, and of the fact that "nothing stands in the way of a separation, the matrimonial yoke sits easily and lightly, and a Typee wife lives on very pleasant and sociable terms with her husbands" (p. 192). There is also a special dispensation for many of the chiefs, who spend a good deal of time away from home. "In truth, Mehevi seemed to be the president of a club of hearty fellows, who kept 'Bachelor's Hall' in fine style at the Ti . . . . and . . .they allowed no meddlesome housekeepers to turn topsy-turvy those snug little arrangements they had made" (pp. 189-190). Yet Mehevi seems to be married, and to have a child by "one of the prettiest little witches in the valley" (p. 190). This lackadaisical husbandly posture within the already flexible Typee social structure is widespread; the men can be absentee husbands—always, in Melville's mind, a situation to be preferred.

If the bonds of matrimony and family responsibility sit lightly on husbands and wives, it is easy enough to see how they effect the children, especially the relations between fathers and their sons. In Typee the conventional Western attitudes toward family life that forge tight bonds of reverence and dependence between parent and child are not present. Since the Typees are a society with families but, by "civilized" standards, without fathers, the separation of a father from a son is much less potentially devastating than it would be in places like nineteenth century Albany or New York City. A Typee son would not have to face the sort of intense emotional disruption at the death of a father that, for instance, young Melville did. Neither would he have to face the social or economic disruptions. The valley is a place where no one has to work, and where poverty as civilization experiences it does not exist because of the surrounding plenitude. For Melville, the essence of this abundance expresses itself most pointedly in the fact that

> [a] gentleman of Typee can bring up a numerous family of children and give them all a highly respectable cannibal education, with infinitely less toil and anxiety than he expends in the simple process of striking a light; whilst a poor European artisan, who through the instrumentality of a lucifer performs the same operation in one second, is put to his wits' end to provide for his starving offspring that food which the children of a Polynesian father, without troubling their parent, pluck from the branches of every tree around them. [P. 112]

Because, from infancy on, the Typee child does not depend on his father for his maintenance, and can pluck his own

security himself "from the branches of every tree," the
child's emotional deportment toward his parent can be independent of economic considerations. The Typee child's
feelings for his father run no risk of being betrayed by any
collapse of family finances.

The powerful appeal of the Typee Valley for Melville
because it does not have a cash-based economy is clearly evident in Tommo's heated remarks on money in chapter 17:

> The term "Savage" is, I conceive, often misapplied, . . .
> when I consider the vices, cruelties, and enormities of
> every kind that spring up in the tainted atmosphere of a
> feverish civilization . . . .
> . . . .
> . . . . One peculiarity [of the natives] that fixed my ad-
> miration was the perpetual hilarity reigning through the
> whole extent of the vale. There seemed to be no cares,
> griefs, troubles, or vexations, in all Typee . . . .
> There were none of those thousand sources of irritation
> that the ingenuity of civilized man has created to mar his
> own felicity. There were no foreclosures of mortgages, no
> protested notes, no bills payable, no debts of honor in
> Typee; no unreasonable tailors and shoemakers, perversely
> bent on being paid; no duns of any description; no assault
> and battery attorneys, to foment discord, backing their
> clients up to a quarrel, and then knocking their heads
> together; no poor relations, . . . no destitute widows . . . no
> beggars; no debtors' prisons; no proud and hard-hearted
> nabobs in Typee; or to sum up all in one word—no
> Money! [Pp. 125-126]

Tommo's tone is rather frenzied here, as if, once he begins his
seemingly endless list of accusations, only the most conscious
control on his part can stop him from luxuriating in his
hatred of every form of degradation caused by money. And
when he spits out that final, joyous phrase, "no Money!",
anyone who knows about the complicated problems of the
Melville family's borrowing procedures—both before and
after Allan's death—must feel the painful personal reference

of Tommo's speech for Melville. For Melville, the loss of the family cash, and the appearance of things like foreclosures, bill collectors, and "hard-hearted nabobs" had been the painful signs of his family's decline, and the withering of the garden of his own youth.

Even though, in a Western sense, Typee is both fatherless and moneyless, Melville still has his *persona* taken in and protected by Mehevi: while the children of Typee may be beyond needing fathers, Melville's protagonist, the product, like himself, of Western life, needs some parental surrogate to provide him with a sense of shelter. Mehevi, the chief of chiefs, rules over a valley where he and his cohorts pass an endless chain of days in which "so seldom do they ever exert themselves, that when they do work they seem determined that so meritorious an action shall not escape the observation of those around" (p. 159). Tommo is a constant visitor at the Ti, where, most of the time, those present only lounge around and eat. Tommo lounges right along with them, invulnerable to either want or criticism. Tommo's sense of security is only compounded by Mehevi's providing him with a second father, Marheyo. Marheyo, though aging and no longer active, is able to live out his dotage in peaceful and noble tranquility. When, at one point, Tommo approaches Marheyo's house, "the superannuated warrior did the honors of his mansion with all the warmth of hospitality evinced by an English squire when he regales his friends at some fine old patrimonial mansion" (p. 96). Tommo, through his connections with Marheyo's household, is an honored guest at the very center of a Polynesian version of Melville's own early childhood memories.

For all its sunny attractiveness, of course, the garden of Typee Valley is somewhat an emotionally ambiguous place for Tommo, as one can assume it was for Melville. Though initially Tommo sought to explain it away, he is increasingly anxious about the Typees' rumored cannibalism, an anxiety caused by the repressed mechanisms in Tommo's psyche that are fighting to regulate his sense of reality. They remind him that the life of the Typees is not and cannot be his life. If he allows himself to fall under the spell of the valley's delightful surface and bury his sense of its abiding difference from his own life—if he lies down at last in some dream of maidens, and flowers, and abundance—where will he be when he wakes up, as he inevitably must? For Melville, repression could never be permanent; Tommo would find himself trapped between lives. He would be neither Typee nor white. Like the Long Ghost of Melville's second novel, he might become only a displaced spectre amid coral and jungle.

Melville is already obviously aware in *Typee* that status and strength cannot be the only tests of suitability for a surrogate father. There must be some cultural base that both father and son can share, a base broader than just benevolence or humanistic feelings. Mehevi, like Marheyo, is, on the whole, benevolent, humane, and aristocratic. Still, because of the cultural gap between the Typees and Tommo, Tommo must always in one way or another be apprehensive about the meanings of their gestures toward him (are they, for instance, as Toby once insinuates, only feeding them so much in order to fatten them for the final slaughter?) A shared cultural identity is the only thing that can provide final and total participation of the son with the father surrogate; however, the acceptance of a cultural system begins at birth and is restrictive. The Typees cannot leave the valley, just as Tommo cannot stop being "Christian." The word "savage" always comes easily to Tommo's lips. Whether or not he means it disparagingly, the use of the term implies that he looks out at the Typees across an inescapably large cultural gulf. Fayaway embodies the same lesson. Here is the ideal chance for love, but Fayaway cannot be released from her society; to even take her out in a canoe Tommo has to openly violate a strict taboo. Her affection for Tommo can only exist within the limits that the valley sets, limits she is perfectly comfortable with, but which Tommo chafes under. And one wonders what Tommo's reaction would be to sharing her sexually with an older chief. Though he may not want it that way, Melville sees that real solutions to problems exist in cultural time and space, not outside it. There is no hole in the universe one can climb through. Tommo's refusal, therefore, to have his face tattooed in chapter 30 precipitates the last series of crises in the book because, by rejecting the tattooing, he rejects any final attempt at assimilation. He may adopt Typee dress—which, significantly, he still chooses to modify to suit his own Western "views of propriety" (p. 121)—but in accepting the tattooing he would accept a permanent confusion of identity. He would, literally, have his face replaced by one that could never really be his. Indeed, when in *Omoo* Tommo comes across Lem Hardy, "a white man, in the South Sea girdle, and tattooed in the face," he "gaze[s] upon [him] with a feeling akin to horror" (p. 27).[2] Thus, even if Tommo did, for a time (tattoos and all), convince himself that he could fully participate in Typee life, he would sooner of later suffer a relapse of civilized instinct, and find himself to be what he considers Hardy, a cultural freak. Better to step away before he does irreversible damage to himself by stopping too long where he will never belong.

The emotional strain that this break with the Typees entails is illustrated in the violence of the book's conclusion, where, still hampered by his wound, Tommo must struggle to make his escape. The last chapter of the novel has been criticized as contrived and anticlimactic: "[it] appears that Melville had said all he wanted to say *before* Tommo's escape, but sensing that his travel book had indeed turned into something of an adventure tale that needed a dramatic ending he tacked one on."[3] If one considers the last chapter in the light of the psychological dynamics of the book, however, it is more significant than it might be given credit for being. The constantly shifting and threatening groups of natives, the final embrace and gift-giving with the ideal family (Marheyo, Kory-Kory, and Fayaway), and the attempted drowning of a hostile native with a boathook, all comprise a turbulent, anxiety-ridden action of escape, an action that reflects the basic pattern of Tommo's emotional tensions: his ambiguous fear of the Typees and the final recognition of the threat they pose to him, coupled with the feeling that within the dangerous fantasy he almost succumbed to was, indeed, some possibility of emotional peace. Tommo's ambivalence can only be resolved by a definitive, adult act of will, symbolized by his passage to the beach and his aggression with the boathook. He will never forget his sojourn in the valley. Yet he recognizes that he had to create distance between himself and those childish instincts Typee so easily played upon in him, a distance he only half-heartedly desired, and that he would give anything to be able to recross with impunity.

> Just beyond the pi-pi, and disposed in a triangle before the entrance of the house, were three magnificent bread-fruit trees. At this moment I can recall to my mind their slender shafts, and the graceful inequalities of their bark, on which my eye was accustomed to dwell day after day . . . . Even now, amidst all the bustle and stir of the proud and busy city in which I am dwelling, the image of those three trees seems to come as vividly before my eyes as if they were actually present, and I still feel the soothing quiet pleasure which I then had in watching hour after hour their topmost boughs waving gracefully in the breeze. [P. 244)

But to allow his narrator to sit his life away musing on the particulars of bread-fruit trees, Melville knew, could never be sanctioned by the male traditions out of which the more socially responsible areas of his own consciousness had evolved.

If, in ending *Typee* the way he had, Melville had his *persona* free himself from a dalliance with a daydream sort of existence, *Omoo* does not demonstrate any positive fruits of that seeming liberation. Rather, *Omoo* shows that it was the dream, the fantasy, that gave Typee Valley and the South Seas its emotional meaning for both Tommo and Melville. Having stripped himself of that dream, what Tommo now

moves toward is the stillnes of a vacuum, the blankness of the
Tahitian wasteland, because the South Seas without its Typee
Valleys could not be a source of psychological nourishment
to Melville's sailor. Though further literary adventuring in
the islands must have seemed a good idea to the practical side
of Melville after *Typee* scored a popular success, more novels
about the South Seas could in fact only be pointless and
desultory post-mortems after Mehevi's valley. As Tommo
says, setting out from Nukuheva on the Julia, "I could
scarcely believe that the same sun now setting over a waste of
waters, had that very morning risen above the mountains and
peered in upon me as I lay on my mat in Typee" (p. 7). The
reader soon discovers that there is no serious engagement for
Tommo in *Omoo* because there is nothing for him to engage
seriously in. The only burdens Melville seems to place on his
narrator are those of maintaining a sense of humor and of being able to drift with situations so that he does not get involved
enough to be hurt.

The empty stasis of the world Tommo sails into in Tahiti is
made obvious by Melville's portrayal of life on the island. It
has reached a zero point, and is unable to go forward or
backward. It can only stand still, waiting for the end.

> [The Tahitians'] prospects are hopeless. Nor can the
> most devoted efforts, now exempt them from furnishing a
> marked illustration of a principle, which history has always
> exemplified. Years ago brought to a stand, where all that is
> corrupt in barbarism and civilization unite, to the exclu-
> sion of the virtues of either state; like other uncivilized be-
> ings, brought into contact with Europeans, they must here
> remain stationary until utterly extinct. [P. 192]

The only seeming solution for this is either to bring Tahiti
totally into the economic world of the nineteenth century or
to allow it to fall back into that state of nature that held sway
before the white man came. The first is not feasible because
by natural temper the Tahitians love novelty but not sus-

tained effort. When, for example, the English opened a factory in Imeeo, the islanders flocked to it to work; in six months, they had all stopped coming. On the other hand, allowing the islands to regress is impossible. It would mean the West's altering its habits of imperialism. Melville shows his doubts over this ever coming to pass by the amount of time he devotes in *Omoo* to the zeal of missionaries, merchants, and governments to "civilize" more primitive peoples. Also, there is a real question whether, having reached the stage of corruption that the natives are in by the time Tommo enters this fallen garden, the Tahitians themselves could reverse direction, even if left alone. The people have built up a monumental lethargy; their rulers are ineffectual and decadent; poverty and their own exploitation of one another have spread into every corner of the island; their old religions have fallen into decay, while their Christian religious fervor is utterly hypocritical. And no matter what, they would still bear the indelible mark of the Westerner's syphillis, "which now taints the blood of at least two thirds of the common people of the island; and, in some form or other, is transmitted from father to son" (p. 191). Tahiti is a nether world where choices of one course of action or another have little significance. Neither the whites nor the Tahitians can do anything; even discussing the possibility seems futile.

As a reflection of the hopelessness of Tommo's surroundings, Melville is careful to stage the novel so that there is also an erosion of any possibility of Tommo being a force for assertive action: Tommo, like his environment, becomes increasingly empty. This begins in the history of Tommo's voyage on the Julia and his confinement in the Calabooza on Tahiti, which takes up the first fifty-one chapters of the book. Almost all of the first twenty-seven chapters are devoted to the derelict condition of the "Jule," the violence of those aboard, and the uncertainty created by the constantly chaotic relationships among the men, the captain, the mate, and the consul at Tahiti. These conflicting forces only frustrate any assertiveness Tommo shows, and from the time he boards the Julia, he is a prisoner of its confusions. For instance, none of his attempts to mediate the mutiny the men engage in, or to keep the ship from being destroyed, are of any consequence. Already severely weakened by his Nukuheva adventures, he finds that the energy he may occasionally muster to try to set the Julia's situation right is simply swallowed up in the general disorder. The final absurdities come at the Tahitian Calabooza, where the crew are "imprisoned" for their shipboard misdeeds. Though officially inmates of this establishment, they are gradually allowed to roam the island at will, until the Calabooza becomes not a jail, but only the most convenient place to return to in order to eat and sleep between their explorations of the island. In fact, they remain at the Calabooza much longer than any legal or even practical consideration dictates, just to harass the consul who put them there, because they are aware of the embarrassment their presence causes him. "Sensible that none of the charges brought against us would stand, yet unwilling formally to withdraw them, the consul now wished to get rid of us altogether; but without being suspected of encouraging our escape" (p. 198). The crew does not want to give him the satisfaction of escaping, and so they stay on, empty men playing at an empty game. At last, Tommo and Long Ghost just slip off one night. Ironically, they must wait until night because they are afraid of being arrested by the natives who do not understand that the consul really wants to let them get away. These events are much different in quality from Tommo's escape from the Typees. There he could act and his actions had some significant consequence in removing him from a dangerous condition of personality. Here he escapes from someone who only wants to get rid of him, but who, if Tommo is caught, will return him to the Calabooza, only to again tacitly encourage him to get away. Thus, Tommo does not escape, so much as he simply decides to drop off the merry-go-round. He makes the only choice he can in an environment where choices seem to have no conclusive meanings attached to them: he becomes a beachcomber, the indolent companion of the even more indolent Long Ghost.

He takes up this occupation with Long Ghost because the doctor has always been the only individual of any status or sophistication within the circle of Tommo's available acquaintances, and so he can provide Tommo with at least some marginal feeling of self-importance. Tommo had chummied with him from the beginning because in large part their relationship is a way for Tommo to publicize his own superiority to the crew he lands with on Tahiti and thus to affirm that no matter how far the orphan has fallen in appearance, he never becomes just part of the common mass. For Melville to ever allow that to happen to one of his narrators would be a denial of his own sense of family background and the pride he always took in it. The difficulty in *Omoo* is that Long Ghost is a rather rag-tag status figure, to say the least. In a world of compromises for Tommo, forming a friendship with Long Ghost is certainly one of the most conspicuous Tommo makes. It is true that on the one hand, he is reminiscent of the cosmopolitan gentility of someone like Allan Melville.

> His early history, like that of many other heroes, was enveloped in the profoundest obscurity; though he threw out hints of a patrimonial estate, a nabob uncle, and an unfortunate affair which sent him a-roving . . . .
> . . . . And from whatever high estate Doctor Long Ghost might have fallen, he had certainly at some time or other spent money, drunk Burgundy, and associated with gentlemen.
> As for his learning, he quoted Virgil, and talked of Hobbes of Malmsbury, besides repeating poetry by the canto, ... He was, moreover, a man who had seen the world . . . . [H]e could refer to an amour he had in Palermo, his lion hunting before breakfast among the Caffres . . . . [P. 12]

But at the same time that he flashes all these glories before Tommo's eyes, he is essentially a man without direction (except the path of least resistance), and, like Tommo, is never capable of energizing any situation into significance. Throughout the book, he practices a kind of vague, benevolent self-gratification, resembling in his shiftless cunning the Tahitian natives: he provides a good laugh for the men in the Calabooza when he succeeds in getting laudanum for them; he charms the planters he and Tommo work for on Martair in order to avoid doing any work; he goes into a faked swoon in the Calabooza, calculated, Tommo suspects, to get him removed from the jail and so "insure more regularity in his dinner-hour" (p. 195).

Together, however, Tommo and Long Ghost can form a pleasant, if shabby aristocracy of two among their comrades.

> Aside from the pleasure of his society, my intimacy with Long Ghost was of great service to me in other respects . . . . [T]he forecastle . . . not only treated him in the most friendly manner, but looked up to him with the utmost deference, besides laughing heartily at all his jokes. As his chosen associate, this feeling for him extended to me; and gradually we came to be regarded in the light of distinguished guests. At meal-times we were always first served, and otherwise were treated with much respect. [P. 36]

Tommo certainly feels for the plight of the seamen. He would have to: he himself is a sailor and so runs the risk of receiving the same punishment and ill-treatment as the others. But the overriding awareness that Tommo has is of his and the Long Doctor's elite position, a position that Tommo is quite unwilling to give up. In fact, when he and Long Ghost receive rather discouraging treatment at the hands of Dr. Johnson, the consul's attendant lord on Tahiti, and so become "to a certain extent, . . . bent on making common cause with the sailors" (p. 83), Tommo takes a paragraph out to make certain that the reader does not misconstrue his action as an assimilation of his personality into the mass of the crew.

> I must explain myself here. All [Long Ghost and I] wanted was to have the ship snugly anchored in Papeetee Bay . . . . Without a downright mutiny, there was but one way to accomplish this: to induce the men to refuse all further duty, unless it were to work the vessel in . . . . Nor was it without certain misgivings, that I found myself so situated, that I must necessarily link myself, however guardedly, with such a desperate company . . . . [Pp. 83-84]

Tommo does not want to be judged by the company he keeps; and it is not just a normal desire to avoid the harsh physical consequences that might ensue. For if people came to associate his habits and attitudes with those of the crew, he would be reduced to a state of being no better than they are, something that would seriously challenge his aristocratic self-image. His need to control the situation aboard ship may in part be simply a benevolent exercise of reason; but it is also a way of protecting his social position.

Just how much of this sort of security he needs is indicated later in the novel, when he shows some irritation over Long Ghost's relationship with Zeke and Shorty, the two Martair farmers. The doctor is a man whose glib tongue and endless stories keep the planters sitting "in mute admiration before him" (p. 231). Zeke and Shorty "counted more upon his ultimate value to them as a man of science, than as a mere ditcher" (p. 231). Long Ghost steals the stage. In Zeke and Shorty's eyes, it is Tommo who is the "mere ditcher." To them, Tommo is no better than they are, and he resents this. He feels his superiority warrants recognition; up until Long Ghost's socially eclipsing him, he found Martair an ideal spot for gratifying his image of himself. He, indeed, had felt that his "society was both entertaining and instructive to a couple of solitary, illiterate men" like Zeke and Shorty (p. 230). He needs, in some way, to be "regarded . . . with emotions of en-

vy and wonder" (p. 230). If this is not forthcoming, he gets a
little sour and a little pettish, and will then reduce himself to
fighting with Long Ghost over who will play the gentleman.

> To tell the plain truth, things at last came to such a pass,
> that I told him, up and down, that I had no notion to put
> up with his pretensions; if he were going to play the
> gentleman, I was going to follow suit; and then, there
> would quickly be an explosion. [P. 231]

Possible loss of status is for Tommo not just an occasion
for annoyance; it is, at one point, an occasion for real shame
and panic. While still a resident at the Calabooza, he is quite
upset at the aversion shown to him by the Europeans on the
Broom Road, conduct that is the result of stories circulated
about the Julia's crew by the consul. This preys on Tommo's
mind and when, in chapter 43, his pleasantries to the wife and
daughter of a missionary are shunted aside, he retreats "in
double quick time; and scarcely drew breath, until safely
housed in the Calabooza" (p. 167). Even though Tommo is
magnanimously willing to admit about the crew that once off
the ship and on shore "better behaved sailors never stepped
on the island" (p. 166), he still gives more emotional credence
to the false and superficial opinions of "respectably dressed
European[s]" (p. 166) than to his own knowledge of the
truth. Being rejected by respectable people creates the fear
that perhaps the orphan sailor has declined further than he
knows.

Of course, for most of the novel Tommo acts in no better
fashion than Long Ghost, who is certainly not a very respectable type. Tommo's behavior hits bottom, however, during
his and Long Ghost's stay in Partoowye. It is here that Tommo comes across Po-Po and his family, a version of the ideal
hosuehold scenes in *Typee*. Po-Po, the head of the family,
"turned out to be a sort of elder, or deacon; he was also accounted a man of wealth, and was nearly related to a high

chief" (p. 280). Po-Po's house is a model of gentility and refinement. Afretee, Po-Po's wife, is courteous and solicitous for their comfort; and Monee, "Po-Po's factotum" (p. 279), is one of the few industrious and capable people Tommo comes across. Lastly, there is a daughter, Loo, who resembles Fayaway in her innocence and freshness, "like a bud just blown" (p. 278). All of these people carry on their lives in an atmosphere of practical piety: at the beginning and end of every day they read from the Tahitian Bible and then pray, while before and after each meal they say grace. "Po-Po was, in truth, a Christian" (p. 280).

One would expect this family grouping to touch Tommo's deepest feelings, but it does not. He is, in fact, indifferent to them. It might perhaps be said that this is a good thing because it demonstrates Tommo's freedom from being lured into the kind of regressive passivity he showed in *Typee*. But if this is so, Tommo is not replacing his penchant for regressive behavior with any purposeful activity. Both Tommo and Long Ghost's only concern is how they can use information Po-Po may be able to given them to become retainers of Queen Pomaree—Tahiti's enervated version of Mehevi—a licentious ruler and the center of a court of politicians and adventurers. Thus, Tommo's lack of concern for Po-Po and his family is only another manifestation of the withering of his ability to generate intense emotions about anything during his travels through Tahiti. Tommo, once a loving member of Marheyo's household in Typee Valley and a friend of one of the greatest of chiefs, looks on Po-Po mainly as an expedient toward becoming an understrapper to a deteriorating queen. And if Po-Po cannot provide them with enough encouragement about the prospects of becoming retainers to Pomaree, they will simply go and seek out others: "We concluded to kill time in Partoowye, until some event turned up more favorable to our projects" (pp. 287-288). "To kill time" is a very appropriate phrase to describe the adventures of a nar-

rator who disregards households such as Po-Po's in favor of
jokesters like Long Ghost and a Tahitian aristocracy in the
last stages of decline.

Tommo can even be indifferent to Long Ghost's attempt to
seduce Loo by faking an interest in the Bible she is reading.
Long Ghost disrupts the basic pattern of the family life in Po-
Po's household and uses religion in the same hypocritical way
the Tahitians do all through the book. But while Tommo had
been critical of the Tahitians' hypocrisy, and had been in-
censed at the Western sexual exploitation of Polynesian
natives symbolized by the prevalence of syphillis, he does not
react to Long Ghost's conduct at all. "I am pretty sure that
Loo must have related this occurrence to her father, who
came in shortly afterward; for he looked queerly at the doctor. But he said nothing; and, in ten minutes, was quite as af-
fable as ever" (p. 294). Tommo's only concern here, as Long
Ghost's has been all the way through the novel, is affability.
He can stand by and sanction, through his good humor, both
seduction and hypocrisy as long as no one gets mad.
Tommo's rejection on the Broom Road seemed to him a
painful case of mistaken identity; but perhaps the respectably
dressed Europeans were right in keeping him at arm's length.

Fortunately, Melville could not allow his narrator to continue indefinitely in this way. For a while, he can have Tommo accept Long Ghost so readily because Melville himself is
so tired and empty after *Typee,* so dispirited, like Tommo, by
the prospect of the real world outside the fantastic Typee
garden, that it is difficult for him to do anything else. But for
a personality as turbulent as Melville's, the ethics of exhaustion—the humorous avoidance of serious choices or emotions—can only be a temporary way out of resolving its conflicts. As D. H. Lawrence pointed out:

[Long Ghost] was a man of humorous desperation, throwing his life ironically away . . . .
. . . .
But it wasn't enough. The Long Doctor was really

knocking about in a sort of despair. He let his ship drift rudderless.

Melville couldn't do this. For a time, yes . . . . But a man who will not abandon himself to despair or indifference cannot keep it up.[4]

Newtown Arvin was also aware that Melville's proper direction was not Long Ghost's:

. . . in confronting. . .antinomies head-on and, hopefully, transcending them—in that direction, as Melville intuitively saw, lay his right future as an adult person. The alternative was a lifetime of raffish vagrancy with the seedy Long Ghost, and a kind of Conradian dilapidation at the end.[5]

So, shortly after their visit to Partoowye, Tommo and Long Ghost part company. Long Ghost, lacking the residue of male responsibility that pushes Tommo to finally break the monotonous cycle that has been their beachcomber existence, merely folds himself back into the vacuous life of an island wanderer. Tommo takes ship, but the doctor "did not quite relish the idea of occupying a position so humble [as that of a sailor]. In short, he made up his mind to tarry awhile in Imeeo" (p. 315). On this vague gesture we see the last of Long Ghost. The final feeling of the book is impulse, movement, escape, the urge in Melville toward assertive behavior. "Crowding all sail, we braced the yards square; and, the breeze freshening, bowled straight away from the land. Once more the sailor's cradle rocked under me, and I found myself rolling in my gait" (p. 316). The sun is not setting, as it was in chapter 1, over a "waste of waters" (p. 7); when Tommo leaves Tahiti, "the dawn showed itself over the mountains" (p. 316). There is the herald of something new, something to be expected. Melville resurrects both his protagonist and himself from possible collapse. Certain instincts, however dormant, never cease to function, and can sometimes hold one on course.

Notes

1 .Harrison Hayford, Hershel Parker, and G. Thomas Tanselle, eds., *Typee* (Evanston and Chicago: Northwestern University Press and the Newberry Library, 1968).

2. Harrison Hayford, Hershel Parker, and G. Thomas Tanselle, eds., *Omoo* (Evanston and Chicago: Northwestern University Press and the Newberry Library, 1968).

3 .Donald E. Houghton, "The Incredible Ending of Melville's *Typee*," *Emerson Society Quarterly* 22 (1961):31.

4. D. H. Lawrence, *Studies in Classic American Literature* (New York: Doubleday and Co., Inc., 1951), pp. 152-153.

5. Newtown Arvin, *Herman Melville* (New York: William Sloane Associates, 1950), p. 88.

3

Women: *Mardi* and *Pierre*

WOMEN are only a very casual part of the landscapes of *Typee* and *Omoo:* delightful, but essentially trivial and decorative. The relationships of importance occur betwen Tommo and other males. *Mardi,* however, is conspicuous among Melville's three adventures of the South Seas because of the dominance of its narrator Taji's single-minded pursuit of the idealized Yillah. The reason for this shift in emphasis was certainly Meville's courtship and marriage with Elizabeth Shaw during the book's composition. "He and his fiancée had probably read both *Undine* and its companion piece, *Sintram and His Companions,* together before their marriage: and the continued allegory of the story was made up of suggestions derived from these two German romances, from Spenser's *Faerie Queene,* and from Elizabeth's books of flower symbolism."[1] But even so, it should not be assumed that the quest for Yillah was some private form of lover's literary communication from Herman to Lizzie, the woman who "shared his hopes . . ., kept his inkwell filled and his paper in order, and prized the hour at the end of the day when he would read the result of his labors aloud to her."[2] In fact, the curious thing about the Yillah material is that it does not seem to be an extension or expression of enthusiasm on

Melville's part for his new wife or for his condition as husband, but rather of a desire for freedom from both. *Mardi,* as a result, resembles less some fictional garden of true love's glories, than it does a battlefield for deepseated ambivalences in Melville over familial and even sexual matters that his marriage appears only to have exacerbated rather than resolved. *Mardi,* perhaps, is one of the best explanations of why Melville's sailors always remained bachelors, and why, after *Mardi,* Melville returned, in quick succession, to three novels dominated by the all-male atmosphere of ships.

To begin with, the marked difference between the social context of Melville's relation to Lizzie, and that of his narrator Taji's relation to Yillah, argues that Taji and Yillah served Melville as a surrogate romance intended to compensate him for certain elements lacking in his own life with Elizabeth. Melville's marriage was consummated within the framework of already existing family connections and traditions. His wife was the daughter of an old family acquaintance and benefactor (the Judge had been an executor of Allan Melville's will), and Elizabeth was also a good friend of his sisters, to whom Melville was always especially attached, as he was to his mother. Marrying her, therefore, constituted no movement beyond established relationships; it was simply a reinforcement of what the passive part of his personality was already comfortably and securely used to. At the same time, however, it was just the sort of marrying among socially connected families usually done by his Dutch relatives (albeit in their case for reasons of commercial consolidation). Thus, on the one hand, he could imagine himself, in his own fashion, playing out an expected form of responsible male behavior, while at the same time he was able to keep the child in himself surrounded by women, and also to put that child in a position of more available proximity to the paternalism of Judge Shaw.

But no matter how much of a perfect compromise for Melville's divided spirit this marriage might seem to have been, the context that Melville provides for Taji's romance with Yillah seems to show that Melville's personality at its deepest levels was not satisfied with the bond between himself and Elizabeth. Taji is free to sail the Mardian archipelago without impediment, moving through a world where he is related to no one, and has no obligations to anyone but himself. His coming together with Yillah is not the end product of relationships imposed by evolving social circumstances in his life; it is the result of an act of spontaneous heroism. And the act is the murder of a powerful male of special status, Aleema, just the sort of individual that Melville in his own life so often resorted to depending on. Aleema, interestingly enough, is chief priest on the island of Amma, as Lemuel Shaw was Chief Justice of Massachusetts. Melville, the acquiescent son-in-law, dreams in the pages of his new novel about a murder that would not only free his narrator's potential bride irrevocably from her "father," but would also establish his narrator's own total independence from any male but himself, no matter how strong. And once Yillah is removed from Aleema's sphere of influence, Taji can begin a life with her alone, in the secluded islet bower off Odo, not, as Melville found himself with Elizabeth, in a crowded household in New York, or the Shaw home in Boston to which Elizabeth so regularly returned. In marrying Elizabeth, Melville had stolen no fairy maiden from her captor; he had, indeed, himself been captured. Taji, on the other hand, desires to withdraw into a life denied to Melville, one where he can inhabit a tranquil paradise without thoughts of responsibility of any sort. It would be superior even to Typee Valley because he and Yillah would be the only people present: no social or cultural identities to get in the way of their total enjoyment of one another. It would constitute the ultimate liberation into a state of regressive repose. Taji fights hard to get and to keep Yillah; he even becomes desperately self-assertive when he begins to understand he will never have her—but all these aggressive gestures have as their source and purpose not Taji's involvement with the world, but his desire to utterly extricate himself from it. As a child so often does, he would prefer to live in the privacy of a world made by himself for himself, where family, culture, economics, and any other "adult" realities are completely put aside. As long as these adult things remain present, even if one has somehow arranged one's life to minimize their negative influences (as Melville often tried to do), they are still reminders of one's bondage to a life of constant compromise and unfulfilled dreams.

Yillah, as a result, does not represent in Taji any urge to come together with a real woman possessing an articulated identity and actual connections to an actual world, but rather the need to find some pliable female form onto which he can project his own visionary desires. It is Yillah's convenient anonymity (she is only what she can be made by others, like Aleema) that draws the narrator so strongly to her. Taji has always looked on external reality with a combination of boredom and distrust; very early in the novel he turns his eyes from the weary and monotonous everyday facts of shipboard life on the Arcturion, and directs his imagination toward the "dreamland" landscape of the western horizon, his mind bounding out into waves of endless space, movement, and sound, lodging finally in the shelter of an island garden.

In the distance what visions were spread! The entire western horizon high piled with gold and crimson clouds; airy arches, domes, and minarets; as if the yellow, Moorish sun were setting behind some vast Alhambra. Vistas seemed leading to worlds beyond. To and fro, and all over the towers of this Nineveh in the sky, flew troops of birds. Watching them long, one crossed my sight, flew through a low arch, and was lost to view. My spirit must have sailed in with it; for directly, as in a trance, came upon me the cadence of mild billows laving a beach of shells, the waving of boughs, and the voices of maidens, and the lulled beatings of my own dissolved heart, all blended together. [Pp. 7-8][3]

Later, Yillah becomes for Taji only the embodiment of the
island he imagined, as he readily molds her into the image of
his own profoundest longings. In chapter 46, for example, he
is content to drift with her at sea, because she is, in fact, the
only "land" he needs.

> Besides, what cared I now for the green groves and
> bright shore? Was not Yillah my shore and my grove? my
> meadow, my mead, my soft shady vine, and my arbor? Of
> all things desirable and delightful, the full-plumed sheaf,
> and my own right arm the band? Enough: no shore for me
> yet. One sweep of the helm, and our light prow headed
> round toward the vague land of song, sun, and vine: the
> fabled South. [P. 145]

Yillah's role is to provide Taji with a mechanism of constant
epiphany, a way of luxuriating in the attention of a female
who reinforces his perpetual egotism in which he reconstructs
the things around him to become merely adjuncts to his imagination.

And so, Melville's actual early married life moved on in
predictable and unromantic channels[4] while, through Taji, he
pursued Yillah. Lizzie, after all, could never be simply
anonymous clay to be turned to whatever dreamy shapes
Melville's heart might ideally crave, and so, her principal
function during Herman's work on *Mardi* was to help control
his domestic environment so that his mind could feed on itself
at his desk. Elizabeth's description of the organiztion of a
typical day in the Melville household shows that it was her
duty to see that the routine Melville had set up for his writing
activities (and even his nonwriting activities) was sedulously
followed in order to maintain a situation in which he could
spend the most time sailing with Taji after Yillah.

> . . . We breakfast at 8 o'clock, then Herman goes to walk
> and I fly up to put his room to rights, so that he can sit
> down to his desk immediately on his return. Then I bid him
> goodbye with many charges to be an industrious boy and

not upset the inkstand, and then flourish the duster, make the bed, etc., in my own room. Then I go downstairs and read the papers a little while, and after that I am ready to sit down to my work—whatever it may be—darning stockings—making or mending for myself or Herman—at all events, I haven't seen a day yet, without *some* sewing or other to do. If I have letters to write, as is the case today, I usually do that first—but whatever I am about, I do not much more than get thoroughly engaged in it, than ding-dong goes the bell for luncheon. This is half-past 12 o'clock—by this time we must expect callers, and so must be dressed immediately after lunch. Then Herman insists upon taking a walk every day of an hour's length at least. So unless I can have rain or snow for an excuse, I usually sally out and make a pedestrian tour a mile or two down Broadway. By the time I come home it is two o'clock and after, and then I must make myself look as bewitchingly as possible to meet Herman at dinner. This being accomplished, I have only about an hour of available time left. At four we dine, and after dinner is over, Herman and I come up to our room and enjoy a cosy chat for an hour or so—or he reads me some of the chapters he has been writing in the day. Then he goes down town for a walk, looks at the papers in the reading room etc., and returns about half-past seven or eight. Then my work or my book is laid aside, and as he does not use his eyes but very little by candle light, I either read to him, or take a hand at whist for his amusement, or he listens to our reading or conversation, as best pleases him. For we all collect in the parlour in the evening, and generally one of us reads aloud for the benefit of the whole. Then we retire very early—at 10 o'clock we all disperse—indeed we think that quite a late hour to be up.[5]

A significant part of Melville's view of his wife's relation to him during this time may be embodied in the figure of Jarl, because her role as helpmate and regulator very closely resembles the role Melville has Jarl play in relation to Taji early in the novel. While he and Jarl are adrift at sea, Taji prefers to commune with himself in the stern of the Chamois and leave the running of the boat to Jarl, who, in addition to his nautical duties, sews Taji's clothes, attends to Taji's meals, and generally devotes himself to Taji in a subservient, spouse-like fashion: in a paraphrase of the Christian marriage ceremony, Taji even comments that Jarl "loved me; from the first [he] had cleaved to me" (p. 13). It would be pressing the matter too hard to say that Melville consciously had his own expectations of Elizabeth in mind when he created Jarl for Taji, but it is significant that the duty that Melville feels is the one most appropriate to Jarl—that of keeping Taji free from everything but his own thoughts—is precisely the major duty Melville required of Elizabeth. And if the analogy between Taji's chummy and Melville's bride seems plausible, it is significant, too, that whatever affection Taji bears for Jarl because of what he does for him is almost completely forgotten once Yillah hails into view. Neither Jarl nor Elizabeth could finally compete in Melville's imagination with an emotional abstraction like Yillah, a fantasy figure embodying the perpetual arrestment of the most intense period of romantic courtship as Taji describes it in chapter 26: "when men's mouths are honey-combs: and, to make them still sweeter, the ladies the bees which there store their sweets; when fathomless raptures glimmer far down in the lover's fond eye" (p. 84). In the usual course of courtship and marriage, Taji goes on to say, that intensity is only possible in temporary ways, and only when "visits are alternated by absence" (p 84). Love, as most people experience it, cannot bear too much familiarity, and "all . . . philosophy about wedlock is not proof against the perpetual contact of the parties concerned" (p. 84). This is a gloomy perspective for Melville's *persona,* and suggests the consciousness on Melville's part of something essential already lost in his own marital situation (perhaps even something he discovered had been doomed all along never to exist). Just as Taji drops out of the real world of his ship, the Arcturion, guided only by the unregulated impulses of his own imagination, it is as if Melville, while still ostensibly in the process of settling down with Elizabeth, had in fact begun to emotionally desert her for another "woman," one with whom familiarity could only breed more and more intense affections.

Part of this desertion may also have had its roots in sexual confusion on Melville's part (not, indeed, an unknown reaction in new husbands, though the evidence seems to be that Melville did not outgrow it). Taji, after all, frantically chases a girl of high and lovely virginity, while being in turn chased by Hautia, who seeks to destroy the tranquil purity he tries to establish for himself and his essentially asexual bride. Taji's increasing confusion over the tension created in him by Hautia's attempt to undermine sexually his commitment to Yillah most likely portrays Melville's own anxieties: his fear of sexual surrender, and his bewilderment generally over the idea of physical involvement with women. When, in chapter 194, Hautia finally succeeds in getting Taji alone, there is passion's allure, but it is superseded by empty and terminal dread.

> . . . Hautia glided near;—zone unbound, the amaryllis in her hand. Her bosom ebbed and flowed; the motes danced in the beams that darted from her eyes.
> "Come! let us sin, and be merry. Ho! wine, wine, wine! and lapfuls of flowers! let all the cane-brakes pipe their flutes. Damsels! dance; reel, swim, around me:—I, the vortex that draws all in. Taji! Taji!—as a berry, that name is juicy in my mouth!—Taji, Taji!" and in choruses, she warbled forth the sound, till it seemed issuing from her syren eyes.
> My heart flew forth from out its bars, and soared in air; but as my hand touched Hautia's, down dropped a dead bird from the clouds. [P. 650]

This dread is true of much of the imagery in Taji's Flozellan stay, be it the enticing flowers that are suddenly covered with wasps (p. 645), or the water, full of "rainbow hues," but revealing beneath the bleached bones of dead men (p. 645). There is a numbing fear for Taji at the heart of the sensuality that Hautia holds out to him; his only safety can be in the return of the presence of Yillah, with her innocence like the "meek and blushing morn!/ . . . her pensive eyes the stars,/ That mildly beam from out her cheek's young dawn!" (p. 560).

Too much is sometimes made of Melville's occasional sexual humor in his fiction, as if it indicated Melville was really quite unembarrassed by man's sexual nature and vagaries. *Mardi* implies that, at base, Melville's attitude toward phsyical love was dichotomous and fearful. Taji distrusts passion, distrusts what he thinks of as its darkness, believing that sexual activity demeans the one who allows himself to succumb to it. He is driven into suicidal frenzies over the struggle between passion and purity that his contact with the women in the novel engages him in. Women introduce into his life contradictory emotions that are unresolvable, and that finally split apart his soul. Women become a source of frightening destructiveness, and their terrible power is that they are the vessels of the complexities of love.

As a sailor, of course, Melville never had to confront this; he could remain apart from it. Regardless of the boisterous heterosexuality of his shipmates in port, or their occasional secret homosexuality aboard ship, the representation of the seaman's life in Melville's fiction shows that Melville viewed it as always pleasantly asexual. But in courting and marrying, Melville was inescapably part of a situation where he could not avoid the ambiguous interpenetration of sexual and platonic love, where these seemingly polar realities not only coexisted in the same relationship, but actually nourished one another in a symbiosis utterly confounding. Melville, therefore, was quite probably sympathetic to Taji's difficulties in chapter 191 in more than simply an abstract or literary way.

But how connected were Hautia and Yillah? Something I hoped; yet more I feared. Dire presentiments, like poisoned arrows, shot through me. Had they pierced me before, straight to Flozella would I have voyaged; not waiting for Hautia to woo me by that last and victorious temptation. But unchanged remained my feelings of hatred for Hautia; yet vague those feelings, as the language of her flowers. Nevertheless, in some mysterious way seemed Hautia and Yillah connected. But Yillah was all beauty, and innocence; my crown of felicity; my heaven below;—and Hautia, my whole heart abhorred. Yillah I sought; Hautia sought me. One, openly beckoned me here; the other dimly allured me there. Yet now was I wildly dreaming to find them together. But so distracted my soul, I knew not what it was, that I thought. [P. 643]

It appears that Melville had in Elizabeth his first real shock of discovery that, as a wife, a woman could be a seeming angel of purity and model of safe domestic solicitude, while at the same time being a willing participant in, and temptation to, what Melville felt were the destructive turmoils of sexuality. This could certainly be the specific reference for Melville of Taji's speculation that Yillah and Hautia are one. Also, Melville, with regard to himself, may have found that while his own relation to Lizzie could outwardly be thought of as most untainted, their marriage was still able to tap in him what he considered a shameful core of physical appetite that he had never fully discerned before. For example, when Hautia first appears to Taji and Yillah, she is associated for him with the "tower-shadowed Plaza of Assignations at Lima" (p. 186), an image rife with innuendoes of covert sexuality. Hautia seems to Taji to pry into his very soul, seeing things there he does not want to admit, perhaps even turning up for view some sexual underside to his motives in taking Yillah away from Aleema. This guilt, symbolized both by Hautia, and by the recurring visions of the dead Aleema's face floating in the water wherever Taji goes, only deepens throughout the novel. Finally, in the concluding chapters, he becomes self-destructive, death appearing to be the only way he can cling unchallenged to his sense that an asexual relation to a woman is somehow possible.

In trumpet-blasts, the hoarse night-winds now blew; the

Lagoon, black with the still shadows of the mountains, and the driving shadows of the clouds. Of all the stars, only red Arcturus shone. But through the gloom, and on the circumvallating reef, the breakers dashed ghost-white.

An outlet in that outer barrier was nigh.

"Ah! Yillah! Yillah!—the currents sweep thee oceanward; nor will I tarry behind.—Mardi, farewell!—Give me the helm, old man!"

"Nay, madman! Serenia is our haven. Through yonder strait, for thee, perdition lies. And from the deep beyond, no voyager e'er puts back."

"And why put back? is a life of dying worth living o'er again?—Let *me*, then, be the unreturning wanderer. The helm! By Oro, I will steer my own fate, old man.—Mardi, farewell!"

. . . .

"Now, I am my own soul's emperor . . . ." [P. 654]

Taji, therefore, will sacrifice anything for what he conceives of as the perfect marriage: one set in a context of complete personal freedom, and in which the presence of the wife would not drag the husband or herself into the fearful engagement in pleasures of the flesh.

Anything less than that perfection may also too easily become like the relationship of Samoa and Annatoo, whose story seems to function principally in the novel as a cautionary tale to prospective bridegrooms. Taji comes across this curious man and wife when he and Jarl board the seemingly deserted ship, Parki, in chapter 19. The most memorable moments in Melville's history of their marriage are taken up with the woman, Annatoo, and Melville creates in her a picture of wifehood that is sour in the extreme and a picture of marriage that is frightening to contemplate. Annatoo is both greedy and wasteful. Before Taji and Jarl even board the Parki, she has ransacked it, hoarding and hiding from her husband whatever she finds. Their marriage is "one long campaign, whereof the truces were only by night" (p. 75). Even these truces cease as the chapters go on, and as Annatoo's greed becomes increasingly paranoid.

A few days passed: the brigantine drifting hither and

thither, and nothing in sight but the sea, when forth again on its stillness rung Annatoo's domestic alarum. The truce was up. Most egregiously had the lady infringed it; appropriating to herself various objects previously disclaimed in favor of Samoa. Besides, forever on the prowl, she was perpetually going up and down; with untiring energy, exploring every nook and cranny; carrying off her spoils and diligently secreting them. Having little idea of feminine adaptations, she pilfered whatever came handy:—iron hooks, dollars, bolts, hatchets, and stopping not at balls of marline and sheets of copper. [P. 80]

She has lost whatever ideal womanliness she may have possessed ("having little idea of feminine adaptations"), and is on the brink of destroying everyone on board. Fortunately, in a stroke of poetic justice, she is swept overboard by a violent storm, the chaos of the sea obliterating the chaos of her personality.

But she remains in the book long enough to give one a rather grim look at Melville's only version in *Mardi* of the conventionally married female—ill-mannered, voracious, secretive, subversive, fraught for the male with every danger imaginable. Part of Melville seems to view marriage as an inevitable combat, where the woman, from some unidentifiable frustration over her lot, can too easily become withdrawn and possessive, even turn predator. Melville also seems to be portraying a sense of men's hopeless inadequacy in the face of women. The scenes on the Parki imply that somehow the male cannot satisfy the deepest and most frustrated wishes of the female; indeed, he most often cannot even guess at what they really are. There is always some desire beyond any but her own ken.

Verily, her ways were as the ways of the inscrutable penguins in building their inscrutable nests, which baffle all science, and make a fool of a sage.
Marvelous Annatoo! who shall expound thee? [P. 102]

The best Melville seems to be able to do to compensate for that male inadequacy is to create Samoa as a figure of forebearance, and (even though he is missing an arm) of male grace. "[Y]ou would have thought he had been born without [the arm]; so Lord Nelson-like and cavalierly did he sport the honorable stump" (p. 99). But while all likeable males in Melville assert themselves largely through this same sort of grace, it is clear in *Mardi* that physical presence is too little to throw into the breach against the massive and unspecific agitation of the female. Samoa, for example, was most clear-headed and commanding as he almost single-handedly defeated the Cholos who had attacked the Parki at the Pearl Shell Islands. Melville shows that in the manly and unambiguous world of combat, Samoa's life is not only exciting, but gratifying. In the internecine marital warfare with Annatoo, however, he is involved always in a struggle where the winners and the losers cannot be told apart, where marriage erodes his male identity. This is perhaps why, in the middle of the Parki chapters, Taji pauses to hold up at length as a model of right-minded male conduct that great bachelor warrior, the Indian swordfish. With his grand phallic blade perpetually at the ready, and with no wife to hinder him, he lives a "right valiant and jaunty Chevalier" (p. 104). Taji is indeed quite proud that he once captured a swordfish's bill, and "hung that rapier over the head of [his] hammock" (p. 105) in, no doubt, reverence of so evident a representation of the male principle unhampered. Annatoo, unfortunately, cares nothing for these sorts of gestures and talismens, and surprises Taji by her contempt even of his presence. As he so understatedly recognizes, "women are less apt to be impressed by a pretentious demeanor, than men" (p. 92).

Perhaps the best summary image in *Mardi* of Melville's idea of marriage occurs at the wedding ceremony Taji attends on Mondoldo in chapter 99, where the Edenic trappings only serve to hide a depressing reality. The bride and groom are

decked with flowers but the groom is also tied with cords attached to a great stone. The symbolism is obvious. It may be
true, as Taji says, that "not all nuptials in Mardi were like
these" (p. 302); but Melville does not present any of the other
ceremonies, nor any realistic alternatives to Samoa and Annatoo. Certainly not Yillah, so passive and psychologically
vacant, so much an abstraction through which Melville vainly
sought to deny human sexuality and the actual complexities
of the female personality.

Because Melville made no attempt to understand women,
they remained for him a fortress of perilous approach. Indeed, the three novels that followed Mardi, in their exclusive
focus on shipboard life, show that Melville probably would
have been quite content to never write about women again.
But the period of late 1851–early 1852 created special
pressures that led him, once more, to fictionally play out his
fear and distrust of females, this time in Pierre. It is his only
other book in which women play a crucial part, and it is
merely an extension of the confusion that underlay Mardi.
The names of the women have changed, but the roles they
play vis-a-vis Melville's protagonist remain the same: Mrs.
Glendinning, Lucy, and Isabel become simply later versions
of Annatoo, Yillah, and Hautia.

In November of 1851, Hawthorne had moved away from
the vicinity of Pittsfield and Arrowhead, all but concluding
his famous friendship with Melville, and Melville was alone,
perhaps more so than he had been since his father had died.
Melville had been ecstatic over Hawthorne's presence;
Hawthorne had been the ultimate chummy, the sort of companion soul Melville's sailor boys sought for so often but
could so rarely find. Melville's letters to him are frantic
deluges of love, of the need for approval, of self-promotion
and self-doubt.[6] In short, the insecure child in Melville came
springing forth and leaped right into the lap of the somewhat
reserved (and probably embarrassed) Hawthorne. Hawthorne,

whatever his feelings for Melville, could never meet him on an equal emotional footing: he could not love Melville with that bottomless devotion Melville lavished on him. And one day he was simply gone. What Melville seems to have imagined this left him with is implied by what he chose to write about in *Pierre:* a tortured life, surrounded by women. The loss of Hawthorne apparently brought on a new access of his fear of being abandoned among those creatures who seemed so attractive, but were only capable of knotting his life beyond any sanity.

Pierre is the prospective inheritor of his family lands and of the "proudest patriotic and family associations of the historic line of Glendinning" (p. 5).[7] He has, however, been content to rest passively within this tradition, enveloped by his mother's stifling presence, and by the asexual affection of Lucy Tartan, of whom his mother heartily approves because Lucy, like Pierre, "is docile—beautiful, and reverential, and most docile" (p. 20). He would also like to have a sister, were that possible; he "mourn[s] that so delicious a feeling as fraternal love had been denied him" (p. 7). Thus, though Pierre's grandfather was a hero (like General Gansevoort), and his father was a cosmopolite (like Allan Melville), now that they are both dead, Pierre's imagination would be most content with a household like Melville's had been in 1847 in New York, full of mothers, and wives, and sisters, where a child may have a chance of resting in blissful feminine solicitude. At the same time, Pierre cannot help but feel some stirrings of his family history; and so, when he thinks of having a sister, he sees her as " 'someone whom I might love, and protect, and fight for, if need be. It must be a glorious thing to engage in a mortal quarrel on a sweet sister's behalf!' " (p. 7.). In this way he might be surrounded by women but also live up to the heroic masculine image represented by his grandfather's military baton that hangs on the wall. This would be a faint-hearted compromise, much like Melville's own compromises in these matters, but Pierre would at least perhaps avoid the contradictions of his usual utter passivity, contradictions even his mother is aware of, though she, for her own purposes, is content to let them stand.

> "This is his inheritance—this symbol of command! and I swell out to think of it. Yet but just now I fondled the conceit that Pierre was so sweetly docile! Here sure is a most strange inconsistency! For is sweet docility a general's badge? and is this baton but a distaff then?—Here's something widely wrong . . . ." [P. 20]

Pierre, of course, gets his chance for a "mortal quarrel," but is cruelly destroyed in his bid for male asser-tiveness—destroyed, significantly enough, through the agen-cy of the very women he seeks to be among, including the seeming sister he discovers he does have in Book 3. Whatever promises of comfort the female presence may seem to hold out, it is always a source of the heart's dis-ease.

Mrs. Glendinning, for example, is a tyrant and a con-founder of proper familial roles. The havoc she wreaks on Pierre is the psychological equivalent of Annatoo's destruc-tion of the Parki. She seeks to hoard from the rest of the world all her son's affections; and in her coercion of Pierre into the trebly displaced role of lover-brother-courtier, she acts out of a female frustration, which, like Annatoo's, is beyond the ability of any male to really provide for.

> Altogether having its origin in a wonderful but purely fortuitous combination of the happiest and rarest ac-cidents of earth; and not to be limited in duration by that climax which is so fatal to ordinary love; this softened spell which still wheeled the mother and son in one orbit of joy, seemed a glimpse of the glorious possibility, that the divinest of those emotions, which are incident to the sweetest season of love, is capable of an indefinite transla-tion into many of the less signal relations of our many che-

quered life. In a detached and individual way, it seemed almost to realize here below the sweet dreams of those religious enthusiasts, who paint to us a Paradise to come, when etherealized from all drosses and stains, the holiest passion of man shall unite all kindreds and climes in one circle of pure and unimpairable delight. [P. 16]

Interestingly, in this one brief analysis, Melville identifies as the source of a woman's often voracious nature the same experience of the loss of ideality, the same discovery of thorns in the marriage bed, which his males make. Yet Melville's sense of women's dangerousness is so fixed by the time he creates Mrs. Glendinning, that rather than sympathize with her plight, he portrays her as a castrater whose attempts to fill up the empty spaces of her life inevitably produce traumatic consequences for any men close to her.

Lucy Tartan remains, like Yillah, a virginal figure out of a fairy tale, someone whose ideal purity becomes a constantly reproaching whip to Pierre's conscience; while Isabel, his supposed illegitimate sister, serves in the stead of Hautia—the dark woman, a temptation for Pierre toward sexuality. Indeed, Isabel's grotesque and hysterical history, which produces such corresponding hysteria in Pierre, shows Melville's continuing sense that sexuality—of which she is the symbol, and toward which she beckons—produces aberrant and dangerous behavior. Sexuality in *Pierre,* as in *Mardi,* is a form of madness, which only begets more madness in its wake. And Pierre, like Taji, must at last become self-destructive to escape it.

Pierre does try vainly for a time to reverse the process of man's seemingly inevitable decline into sexual depravity. The presumed fruits of his father's own base conduct are passed on to Pierre in the form of Isabel; she becomes the lure for Pierre to repeat the sin his father is believed to have committed with Isabel's mother. But Pierre feels that if he could provide the abandoned Isabel with some sort of true sibling relationship, he could not only save Isabel from her painful past,

he could also save himself; he could decline the gambit of his
father's sin, and so could be free from the fearful notion that
carnality is unavoidable, generation after genertion. As it
turns out, however, he winds up committing his father's sin
over again with Isabel, at least symbolically. Driven half-
crazy by his attempts to sublimate his sexual attraction for
her into ideal brotherly protectiveness, he finally rips open
the bosom of her dress and drinks from a poison vial she
keeps there, showing that he, like Taji, believes that if he
once accepts the necessity of sexuality, then he must in turn
renounce life and happiness. Interestingly, in all of this the
father, though he is morally reproved by Pierre for his conduct, is seen as only the secondary agent of Pierre's fall; it is
the women who are the receptacles for the poison that cor-
rupts so absolutely it can kill.

As one might expect from the attitudes that surface in *Mardi* and *Pierre,* the Melvilles' marriage had a somewhat stormy
passage down the years. There were constant tensions,
sometimes from Lizzie's nerves, but most usually from Herman's: regular bouts with depression and self-recrimination,
accompanied by psychosomatic reactions; alienation from his
children and grandchildren, whom he often felt hated him;
need for constant reassurance and privacy; and an all-
consuming selfishness when readying a book for publication.
The Melville household was a place of failed hopes for Herman, and of a marriage which at times only shakily succeeded
in holding itself together. Recent evidence, for instance, indicates that the Shaws tried, in 1867, to engineer a legal
separation for Elizabeth behind Herman's back because both
they and Lizzie were "convinced that her husband is
insane."[8] "I think she would have done this long ago," wrote
Sam Shaw to Lizzie's minister, Henry Whitney Bellows, "if
not for imaginary and groundless apprehensions of the cen-
sure of the world upon her conduct."[9] While it would certainly be foolish to interpret Sam Shaw's "long ago" as ex-
tending back as far as 1847, one cannot help feeling that the

marital crisis of the 1860s had its origin partly in those conflicts that Melville's marriage originally seemed to bring into
painful concentration for him. The question of the possible
separation was not simply a squall, but a major blow in the
Melville household, the first stirrings of which had touched
Elizabeth's face, ever so gently, when, as a new wife, she had
read to her husband his manuscript pages about Taji's quest
for a love which, in its promise of utter freedom and of an
asexual simplicty of emotional relationships, was the antithesis of what her life with Herman would have to be, what
any woman's life with him would have been.

Notes

1. Leon Howard, *Herman Melville* (Berkeley: University of California Press, 1951), p. 114.

2. Ibid.

3. Harrison Hayford, Hershel Parker, and G. Thomas Tanselle, eds., *Mardi* (Evanston and Chicago: Northwestern University Press and the Newberry Library, 1970).

4. See Howard, pp. 108-111; Eleanor Melville Metcalf, *Herman Melville: Cycle and Epicycle* (Cambridge; Harvard University Press, 1953), pp. 48-55.

5. Metcalf, pp. 48-49.

6. See Merrell R. Davis and William H. Gilman, eds., *The Letters of Herman Melville* (New Haven: Yale University Press, 1960), pp. 118-144.

7. Harrison Hayford, Hershel Parker, and G. Thomas Tanselle, eds., *Pierre* (Evanston and Chicago: Northwestern University Press and the Newberry Library, 1971).

8. Walter D. Kring and Jonathan S. Carey, "Two Discoveries Concerning Herman Melville," *Proceedings of the Massachusetts Historical Society,* 87 (1975):140.

9. Ibid.

4

Redburn, White-Jacket, Moby-Dick:
Full Circle

A S he worked on *Redburn and White-Jacket* during the
months immediately following *Mardi's* publication,
Melville seemed to be making a new beginning for himself.
Taji had been a self-annihilating, self-centered individual;
and his narrative, so obtuse, had caused various readers to
look on Melville's allegorical voyaging as "regrettable."[1] And
so, writing to Richard Bentley, his publisher, in June of 1849
about *Redburn,* Melville indicated that

> I have now in preparation a thing of a widely different
> cast from "Mardi":—a plain, straightforward, amusing
> narrative of personal experience—the son of a gentleman
> on his first voyage to sea as a sailor—no metaphysics, no
> conic sections, nothing but cakes & ale. I have shifted my
> ground from the South Seas to a different quarter of the
> globe—nearer home—and what I write I have almost
> wholly picked up by my own observations under comical
> circumstances . . . .[2]

Melville apparently wanted, after the excesses of *Mardi,* to
begin once again with the construction of a new instance of
that externally acceptable *persona* he had first undertaken to

project in *Typee*. By creating narrators who, unlike Taji, his audience could feel were sensible and credible, he would be able not only to sell books, but also to cultivate with the public an image of himself as responsible rather than eccentric. He could, in effect, organize himself again in the image of expected male behavior that he had grown up surrounded by. And so, Wellingborough Redburn desires to demonstrate to his readers that he has been able to take the first steps toward maturity, even though he had been deeply hurt by the loss of his bankrupt father, and had begun his sea life desperately yearning to return to the emotional safety of his childhood. White-Jacket, on the other hand, presents himself to his audience right from the beginning in full, responsible male regalia. He is intelligent, articulate, knowledgeable, and confines his narrative to the ordinary, observable facts of life in the Navy. In addition, he makes clear his awareness of the necessity for involvement in the affairs of this observable world by using his book, unafraid of intimidation from any quarter, to create a climate of reform in the Navy. He is seemingly willing to do his duty, like General Gansevoort, "to the last extremity."

This strategy on Melville's part with regard to the construction of the personalities of Redburn and White-Jacket did, indeed, work with his public: their narratives temporarily restored his flagging popularity. Unfortunately the evidence is that they did not work with Melville himself in terms of resolving the crisis of identity that had for so long been at the center of his emotional life. He could feel no sense of success from these books so obviously calculated to be successful. In fact, by the time he had the plate proofs for *White-Jacket* in hand, only one week after the English publication of *Redburn,* he had become very bitter over the choice of direction he had imposed on himself. He wrote to Lemuel Shaw:

> For Redburn I anticipate no particular reception of any kind. It may be deemed a book of tolerable

entertainment;—& may be accounted dull.—As for the other book, it will be sure to be attacked in some quarters. But no reputation that is gratifying to me, can possibly be achieved by either of these books. They are two *jobs,* which I have done for money—being forced to it, as other men are to sawing wood . . . . I have felt obliged to refrain from writing the kind of book I would wish to; . . . my only desire for their "success" (as it is called) springs from my pocket, & not from my heart. So far as I am individually concerned, & independent of my pocket, it is my earnest desire to write those sort of books which are said to "fail."—Pardon this egotism.[3]

It is an indication of how painfully wrought up Melville was over this matter that he let his resentment show itself so fully in a letter to his father-in-law. As one of the principal representatives of all those subtle but ever-present family pressures that created for Melville his sense of obligation to the standards of male activity that had been passed down to him, Judge Shaw would be the very individual who would be least sympathetic, especially because of his concern for Elizabeth, to any hints that his son-in-law had not settled down to what could be considered respectable literary conduct. Still, neither the traditions of male accountability that had surrounded his youth, nor any embarrassment over what the Judge might look on as a disregard of mature authorial behavior, could keep Melville from affirming his "egotism"—that tendency on the part of the outraged boy in him to turn his literature inward to feed on its self-indulgences and its rebellious insecurities about its relations to the world of people like Lemuel Shaw.

In retrospect, this reaction of Melville's was predictable because, if one regards *Redburn* and *White-Jacket* with a somewhat more critical eye than their straightforward surfaces appear to demand, one becomes aware that there are in both of them subtexts that belie their narrators' expressions of social maturity. There is a tension in the novels between what Melville would *like to imagine* is possible for Redburn and White-Jacket, and what the configurations of the books themselves tell a reader Melville actually *could believe* was possible. The subtexts indicate that Redburn and White-Jacket, for whatever gains their personalities make over the egotistical and suicidal Taji, are still drifting in an unresolved limbo of identity, unable, as their author was unable, to move beyond their loss of innocence. Melville had forced himself to write these realistic sea novels but he could not, finally, write them in such a way that he could conclusively create a pattern of socially oriented behavior that he could accept and move his narrators on from in subsequent fiction. He had intended to write novels that would help keep under control, in himself and his protagonists, "the certain something unmanageable in us, that bids us do this or that, and be done it must—hit or miss."[4] But even in the very act of trying to do this, he instinctively worked against his intentions, because those intentions could never emotionally suit him.

As a result of this, part of the poignancy of Redburn's tale is that while in it Melville ostensibly fosters the notion that the past need not be one's perpetual prison, he simultaneously demonstrates that, in reality, it will always be one for himself and his sailors. *Redburn* opens with its young hero angry and ashamed at his own feelings of inferiority, waving his gun in the faces of the passengers aboard a Hudson steamer because he cannot pay full passage and cannot bear the looks of others better dressed than he is. Since the novel begins with Redburn's unbearable consciousness of a fall from social and economic grace, one cannot wholly trust his disarming characterization of himself as a boy with "a naturally roving disposition" (p. 3)[5]. It is clear that the death of his cosmopolitan, well-to-do father, Walter Redburn, as a bankrupt, and the subsequent reversals and disappointments it caused Redburn, have put him at loose ends because he has been severed from his father and from the expectations of his youth. In order, therefore, to try to restore some sense of continuity and purpose to his life, he is shipping out to Europe where he hopes to regain an imaginative closeness to his lost father by visiting places his father had visited.

Redburn's early residence in New York City was a time of security and status. Life was quiet; the picture of the world outside was romantically colored by his father's portfolios and art objects. The cosmopolitan nature of his family's assembled home furnishings, and the family's French servant, inevitably breathed to Redburn that he was a gentleman's son. One memory in particular dominates his consciousness, that of a fort on the Narrows that he once visited with his uncle and father, a place he feels epitomizes the gentle security he was able to experience while his father was still alive.

> It was a beautiful place, as I remembered it, and very wonderful and romantic, too, as it appeared to me . . . . On the side away from the water was a green grove . . . . in a sort of twilight you came to an arch in the wall of the fort, dark as night; and going in, you groped about in long vaults, twisting and turning on every side, till at last you caught a peep of green grass and sunlight, and all at once came out in an open space in the middle of the castle. And there you would see cows quietly grazing, or ruminating under the shade of young trees, and perhaps a calf frisking about, and trying to catch its own tail; and sheep clambering among the mossy ruins . . . . [P. 35]

The idealized European landscapes in Walter Redburn's portfolios portrayed the same serenity. And, so, when Redburn looks out to sea in chapter 7, he naturally imagines England made up of "towns and villages and green fields and hedges and farm-yards and orchards, away over that wide blank of sea" (p. 34). What he believes he will encounter in shipping out is very similar to what he feels he is leaving behind; and his mind, in musing about England, reflects his need for it to be like his day on the Narrows.

Considered in this context, it is easy enough to see what the attractions of his dearly loved guidebook, *The Picture of Liverpool,* are for Redburn. The scenes it predicts a traveler will find create visions of the city that combine grandeur with pastoral romance. A poem by a certain Dr. Aiken tells the traveler of the humble fisherfolk who founded Liverpool, *"their nets and little boats their only store"* (p. 147). The city now, of course, is a commercial giant, but Dr. Aiken's verse tries to imply that, at base, it has never lost its idyllic character. A little later on, there is another poem, this time by a "neglected Liverpool poet" (p. 147), a work directed at " *'the cultivated reader; especially as this noble epic* [it tells of Liverpool's dominance in trade] *is written with great felicity of expression and the sweetest delicacy of feeling'* " (p. 147). Redburn is more than ready to relate emotionally to both the poem's intended audience and to its sense of the quality of Liverpool life. First of all, Redburn certainly always considered himself "cultivated"; in fact, he has difficulty initially in coping with his fellow sailors in good part because of his sense of his own superior breeding. Secondly, Redburn welcomes the comfortably vague romanticism of the epic poetry as an anodyne for the harsh realities of sailing before the mast. After the coldness of Captain Riga, the sternness of the officers, the coarseness of the crew, and the general hardship of an ocean voyage, the guidebook poetry is a happy reinforcement of Redburn's image of himself and of those expectations about life abroad that the milieu of his father's house first established for him. The guidebook seems a proof and a promise that the lost world of his childhood feelings is still open to him if he simply puts his trust in the validity of *The Picture of Liverpool.* No wonder Redburn is almost religiously enthusiastic over the book.

The difficulty, of course, is that Redburn keeps running into dead ends when he tries to use the guidebook. He wants to follow his father's footsteps through the city but cannot even locate Riddough's Hotel, from which Walter Redburn launched his own excursion into the town years before, a tour that was a quintessential expression of the secure life-style that Redburn, Sr. enjoyed and that he would presumably have passed on to his son.[6] When Redburn gets to the alleged site of the hotel and finds it has been demolished, he suddenly realizes that *The Picture of Liverpool* cannot reflect a number of specific—and, for him, psychologically crucial—changes in the Liverpool landscape since Walter Redburn's time, and that it never did reflect accurately the general quality of life in the city. Still, Redburn cannot bring himself to throw his father's book away; he has invested too much in it emotionally to ever do that, and it would seem too much like a rejection of his father and of the life his father represented. So, Redburn hopes to minimize his sense of disappointment by trying to hold to a middle ground from which to deal with his feelings: he keeps the book, hoping that in some regards it will still "prove a trusty conductor through many old streets in the old parts" of Liverpool (p. 157), but resolves in the main to explore the city and its environs without the predispositions that the guidebook encourages. He can thereby maintain his reverential attachment to the past (he is always gently stroking the covers of the guidebook, even when it is inaccurate), while convincing himself that he is able to meet the present as it actually exists.

As succeeding incidents show, however, this half-hearted compromise does not work. On his own in the city he sees a dejecting spectacle of death and beggary, and in the countryside around Liverpool he is confronted by "forbidden green fields" (p. 213) that hide "man-traps and spring-guns" (p. 210). His inability to adjust his emotions to these more difficult realities of English life is shown in his wish to withdraw into the country cottage he comes across in chapter 41. "So sweet a place I had never seen: . . . there were flowers in the garden; and six red cheeks [the owner's three daughters], like six moss-roses, hanging from the casement. At the embowered door-way, sat an old man, confidentially communing with his pipe: while a little child, sprawling on the ground, was playing with his shoe-strings" (p. 213). This setting provides Redburn with both an English equivalent of the fort on the Narrows, and a version of the ideal family he craves for himself: a father, safe from financial hazards, living out a comfortable old age in the midst of a pastoral setting, with a child who has nothing to worry about except enjoying the tranquility of his surroundings. And in being drawn instantly to this embodiment of his own fondest dreams, he leaves himself open to the same disappointment he did with the guidebook. Even though he is invited to eat at the cottage, it is made clear to him that he is only regarded as a transient, and is not expected to stay or to try to cultivate the affections of the daughter he particularly has his eye on. He has again, with painful results, allowed himself to fall into the self-deluding mentality of the sea-orphan, believing that he could perhaps once more have a place in a home much like that which his imagination of the past so hungrily doted on, whatever the more realistic part of his personality may tell him. His utter despondency as he goes back into Liverpool, plodding his "solitary way to the same old docks" (p. 215), shows that his attempted compromise with his guidebook was a gesture without real result. He was still, in the deepest and most permanent part of himself, hoping too much to find something somewhere in England that would satisfy the needs that he had brought with him from America. He has remained completely vulnerable to the past; as when his father died, he seems to be facing, on the Liverpool docks, not any definable expectations for the future, but rather an emotional vacuum.

Redburn chooses to fill this vacuum with Harry Bolton, an individual whose principal attraction is that he seems able to provide Wellingborough once more with a continuity of association with his childhood. Harry is the embodiment of everything Redburn believed England at its best would be. To Redburn he seems a figure right out of the sort of financially secure pastoralism he has been seeking proximity to all along.

In chapter 44, for example, Redburn creates a private fantasy in which he portrays to himself Harry's imagined departure from his ancestral home in Bury St. Edmunds.

> In vain did Bury, with all its fine old monastic attractions, lure him to abide on the beautiful banks of her Larke, and under the shadow of her stately and storied old Saxon tower.
> By all my rare old historic associations, breathed Bury . . . . Where will you find shadier walks than under my lime-trees? where lovelier gardens than those within the old walls of my monastery, approached through my lordly Gate? . . . For here, on Angel-Hill, are my coffee and card-rooms, . . . where you may lounge away your mornings, and empty your glass and your purse as you list. [P. 217]

Granted that Harry has told Redburn quite romantic things about his supposed family background and social connections, Redburn's fantasy is still his own, as much a projection of what Redburn needs Harry to be as it is the result of the stories Harry tells. Redburn is therefore prepared to share in Harry's life as he was prepared to share, through the guidebook, in his father's.

Harry, as one might expect, lets him down much the way the guidebook and the cottage did: Harry whisks him off to London, promising to show him the delights of the town, but in fact only leaves him alone all night in the antechamber of a gambling house where Redburn finds himself "alive to a dreadful feeling, . . . never before felt, except when penetrating into the lowest and most squalid haunts of sailor iniquity in Liverpool" (p. 234). And when Harry returns periodically, he is not the smoothly cosmopolitan indvidual Redburn was first attracted to; rather, he is disturbingly frantic and disoriented. Later, aboard ship on the way home, Harry is no more stable than he showed himself to be in London. Though just an ordinary seaman, he dresses foppishly and will not carry out orders, presenting Redburn with an undeniable object lesson about the self-destructiveness of clinging to the past, of trying to persist in attitudes that no longer have any relationship to one's real circumstances.

Redburn, however, cannot take this lesson completely to heart for himself. Regardless of Harry's deceptions in London or his blindess to the necessities of his new life at sea, Redburn takes him under his wing, protecting him on the homeward voyage, and even after the ship makes port. Harry is too deeply associated for Redburn with his own memories of his father and of lost domestic glories to be simply put aside, even though Redburn has a full sight of Harry's essential emptiness and even dangerousness. And so, Redburn can only think to deal with Harry much as he tried to deal with the guidebook: when they arrive back in New York, Redburn turns Harry over to a friend for safekeeping. This allows Redburn to carry Harry nostalgically in his memory, to continue his allegiance to his old modes of feeling, but at the same time to make himself believe that he has achieved some conclusive movement away from the pitfalls of the sort of personality that Harry symbolizes.

It is true that, considered by itself, this final incident can seem, as it does to most commentators, like an eminently reasonable, and even affirmative conclusion to the novel. After all, Redburn, desirous only of engineering a situation that can have happy consequences for both himself and his companion, treats Harry gently and humanely, trying to find for him some occupation more suitable to his talents and physique than that of a common sailor. This affirmative reading of the book is also given support by Redburn's gradual growth in the novel in wisdom about ships and sea usages, and his gradual social integration with the crew he at first felt so alienated from. One cannot deny that Redburn has learned many things on his first voyage. But the fact remains that the form of Redburn's reaction to his most crucial problem—his sense of blight over his lost youth—is essentially repetitive. He is still in the last chapter using the same ineffectual compromise with reality that he had used when he first got to Liverpool. He is unable to let go of what most hurts him. This is also reflected in the circular journey he has taken, returning in the end to his mother and his home, a home empty of the father he so longs to have back again, and presumably still filled with the memories of loss he cannot shake. And even as he writes his narrative, years after his adolescence, and capable of amused detachment about so many of his youthful mistakes, he shows that the wrongs of his childhood created a canker, which, unless it is forcibly repressed, can still cause murderous emotions in him. This is especially noticeable in part of his reminiscences on the Narrows fort.

> And once I saw a black goat with a long beard, and crumpled horns, standing with his fore-feet lifted high up on the topmost parapet, and looking to sea, as if he were watching for a ship that was bringing over his cousin. I can see him even now, and though I have changed since then, the black goat looks just the same as ever; and so I suppose he would, if I live to be as old as Methusaleh, and have as great a memory as he must have had. Yes, the fort was a beautiful, quiet, charming spot. I should like to build a little cottage in the middle of it, and live there all my life . . . . But I must not think of those delightful days, before my father became a bankrupt, and died, and we removed from the city; for when I think of those days, something rises up in my throat and almost strangles me. [Pp. 35-36]

The feelings that the younger Redburn demonstrated on the Hudson steamer toward the passengers are not much different from those of the older Redburn when he is forced to remember his past, and to admit that what he really wants is total regression into a condition of sheltered boyhood. And who is the engimatic black goat, gazing seaward? Possibly some dreamwork projection of Redburn himself, the outcast son, eternally waiting amidst the lost landscape of his past for the one individual who can make that landscape live again, but who never comes? A "cousin," or in reality a father?

Though Redburn can say he has "changed since then," he still seems to carry his old desires and grievances very much intact. It is significant that while he claims to have "passed through far more perilous scenes than any narrated in this, *My First Voyage*" (p. 312), he yet chooses to focus his exclusive attentions on his early life at sea, apparently demonstrating, therefore, that whatever superficial adjustment to his losses he has made, it has brought no satisfying direction to his life. His discovery that he could not continue to live the way he had imagined he could as a child was, perhaps, his ultimate discovery, beyond which he found not new possibilities, but only a constant and disappointing sense of life lived as necessary compromise, a war without victories to keep under tenuous control those emotions that always threatened to ravage him. Whatever surface movement toward an acceptance of his life that Redburn makes, therefore, it is often undercut by the design of the story itself. The reader has precious little evidence that this boy in Melville became a man in the ways Melville's family, or Judge Shaw, would have accepted.

One has the same final impression of White-Jacket, even though, as was noted before, he is himself one of the most seemingly confident of Melville's narrators. White-Jacket speaks to the reader out of an unquestionable familiarity with the nooks and crannies of the "world in a man-of-war," and conceives of his narrative as a historical document calculated not only to shock his contemporaries into moral indignation over abuses in the Navy, but also to project his own voice down through time in ever-new revelations to future generations of readers.

> Let us forget the scourge and the gangway a while, and jot down in our memories a few little things pertaining to our man-of-war world. I let nothing slip, however small; and feel myself actuated by the same motive which has prompted many worthy old chroniclers, to set down the merest trifles concerning things that are destined to pass

away entirely from the earth, and which, if not preserved in the nick of time, must infallibly perish from the memories of man. Who knows that this humble narrative may not hereafter prove the history of an obsolete barbarism? Who knows that, when men-of-war shall be no more, "White-Jacket" may not be quoted to show to the people in the Millennium what a man-of-war was? God hasten the time! Lo! ye years, escort it hither, and bless our eyes ere we die. [P. 282][7]

Yet all of this is not the full reality of his personality. It seems often to be a mask, in fact; for evident in the book also is the Melville sailor in his most childishly dependent phase, eager to revolve around the sun of some more potent male—in White-Jacket's case, Jack Chase. Jack, indeed, remains in both Melville's and White-Jacket's eyes a focus of hero worship even though the eulogistic tone adopted toward him is at variance with certain facts of Chase's personality as it emerges. Jack's weaknesses are overlooked out of the same fascination and desire that made Tommo often overlook Mehevi's cannibalism.

Chase is first introduced in chapter 4.

> Jack was a gentleman. What though his hand was hard, so was not his heart, ... His manners were easy and free; . . . and he had a polite, courteous way of saluting you, if it were only to borrow your knife. Jack had read all the verses of Byron, and all the romances of Scott . . . . Enough, that those accomplishments were so various; the languages he could converse in, so numerous; . . . Jack, he was better than a hundred common mortals; . . . Jack would have done honor to the Queen of England's drawing-room . . . . [P. 14]

Gentlemanly, genteel, literate, and cosmopolitan, Jack embodies all the core qualities of the father who was lost in *Redburn,* and the role Chase plays in White-Jacket's emotional life is as significant a one as Wellingborough's father played in his. The occupation of sailor in Melville, as has been clear throughout his first four novels, always implies social and familial losses; and White-Jacket, whatever his apparent democratic sympathies, is as eager as any of Melville's other protagonists to feel safe and superior. Locked in the floating bastion of the Neversink, where his identity becomes only a set of numbers, and where even teenage midshipmen have legal authority over his person, White-Jacket, day after day, is forced to confront his dissatisfaction at having come so far down in the world and having been made so vulnerable. Chase, however, can supply White-Jacket with the emotional support he needs to reestablish his self-importance, and also to achieve a feeling of insulation from the harsh realities of the deck. The men in the main-top balcony, ruled over by Chase in a thoroughly gentle manner, are not only removed from many of the dangers and denigrations that their ship-mates must face, but they also comprise for White-Jacket a kind of private club—democratic among themselves, but not in relation to the larger life of the ship. In Jack's presence, as in that of Mehevi at the Ti, those whom Jack takes under his benevolent protection become an elite brotherhood. This is quite satisfying to White-Jacket, an individual with a high regard for himself, and a great deal of condescension for the ordinary run of seamen, facts that often undercut his seeming dedication to their welfare.

Be it here, once and for all, understood, that no sentimental and theoretic love for the common sailor; no romantic belief in that peculiar noble-heartedness and exaggerated generosity of disposition fictitiously imputed to him in novels; and no prevailing desire to gain the reputation of being his friend, have actuated me in any thing I have said, in any part of this work, touching the gross oppression under which I know that the sailor suffers. Indifferent as to who may be the parties concerned, I but desire to see wrong things righted, and equal justice administered to all. [P. 304]

From his position in the main-top, White-Jacket can feel the physical elevation he finds necessary to provide himself and his opinions with a corresponding elevation of tone; and much of his wisdom is clearly not egalitarian in content.

> Certain it is, from what I have personally seen, that the English officers, as a general thing, seem to be less disliked by their crews than the American officers by theirs. The reason probably is, that many of them, from their station in life, have been more accustomed to social command; hence, quarter-deck authority sits more naturally on them. A coarse, vulgar man, who happens to rise to high naval rank by the exhibition of talents not incompatible with vulgarity, invariably proves a tyrant to his crew. It is a thing that American man-of-war's-men have often observed, that the Lieutenants from the Southern States, the descendants of the old Virginians, are much less severe, and much more gentle and gentlemanly in command, than the Northern officers, as a class. [P. 141]

White-Jacket may be against corrupt and brutal aristocracies, like that formed by his own captain and commodore on the Neversink, but his alternative is still an essentially elitist one. And he certainly would never entertain giving the ordinary sailor the opportunity to rise to a rank of command. Once more, the reader discovers that Melville's narrators usually only feel outraged at social injustice if they are its potential victims, or if the social injustice attacks their self-image (always, like Melville's own, very vulnerable to external pressures). Otherwise they are, as White-Jacket is, quite content with a hierarchical view of things, especially if they can convince themselves that they occupy a position of significance and safety.

White-Jacket's need to remain aloof with Chase does not change in the course of the book, though Melville does provide an ambiguous gesture at making it seem to change in the quite famous jacket-slashing incident at the book's conclusion. As the narrator's white coat sinks into the sea, he presumably sheds the embodiment of his own sense of difference from those around him, and is born again into the full community of sailors, not just the limited company he has chosen to associate with all through the novel. The problem is that this is symbolic rather than substantial, artificial rather than organic. The incident occurs so close to the book's end that Melville need not be forced to make any concrete demonstration of the attitudinal changes in White-Jacket that the loss of his coat supposedly heralds, changes that Melville was, in fact, probably not totally sympathetic to. It seems only another example of the dichotomy between what Melville felt he should show happening to his narrator, and what he could, in fact, accept as true for his own personality. Like Redburn and Tommo—and Melville—White-Jacket needs, more than anything else, a place to feel loved, protected, and important. Melville is unwilling to take that from him in any conclusive way.

And so, Melville never cuts White-Jacket loose from his apprenticeship to Chase, even when Melville seems aware that Chase's direction, for all its charisma, is not the direction in which meaningfully assertive male action lies. Noble Jack, for example, is never as noble as Melville allows White-Jacket to believe. In the scene in chapter 67 where White-Jacket is about to be flogged, it is not Chase who saves him from final execution of the punishment. It is Colbrook, a corporal of marines, who speaks up in his defense. Though Melville never makes it clear why Colbrook does, he makes clear the courage it took to do so, for Colbrook's "speech was almost unprecedented. Seldom or never before had a marine dared to speak to the Captain of a frigate in behalf of a seaman at the mast" (p. 281). It is only after Colbrook comes forward that Jack takes action on behalf of one of his own men. Even then, he is cautious; and, speaking in a "carefully respectful manner, [he] in substance repeated the corporal's remark, adding that he had never found me wanting in the top" (p. 281). This is a rather weak showing.

Jack repeats the same pattern of behavior later, in an incident involving the seaman, Ushant, a figure of age and reverence among both officers and crew, "a sort of sea-Socrates" (p. 353). Ushant refuses to shave off his beard, and so directly challenges the arbitrary but absolute authority of Captain Claret. For this, like White-Jacket, he is brought forward to be flogged. Jack's first impulse is to threaten violence; but he is finally reduced to impotent tears.

> "Lay on! I'll see his backbone!" roared the Captain in a sudden fury.
> "By Heaven!" thrillingly whispered Jack Chase, who stood by, "it's only a halter; I'll strike him!"
> "Better not," said a top-mate; "it's death, or worse punishment, remember."
> "There goes the lash!" cried Jack. "Look at the old man! By G—d, I can't stand it! Let me go, men!" and with moist eyes Jack forced his way to one side. [P. 365]

The question is whether Jack is truly helpless, or whether, despite his threats, he would never have carried out the rescue of Ushant to begin with. Part of the answer may be contained in a scene just prior to Ushant's flogging, where Jack complies with the order to shave off all beards. Jack will not oppose the system of the ship, but is able to dress up the fact of his submissiveness with an enormous embroidery of bombast.

> My noble captain, Jack Chase, was indignant . . . . But in his cooler moments, Jack was a wise man; he at last deemed it but wisdom to succumb.
> . . . . "Two summers have gone by since my chin has been reaped. I was in Coquimbo then, on the Spanish Main; and when the husbandman was sowing his Autumnal grain on the Vega, I started this blessed beard; and when the vine-dressers were trimming their vines in the vineyards, I first trimmed it to the sound of a flute. Ah! barber, have you no heart? This beard has been caressed by

the snow-white hand of the lovely Tomasita of Tombez—
. . . . Yea, barber! it has streamed like an Admiral's pennant
at the mast-head of this same gallant frigate, the Neversink! Oh! barber, barber! it stabs me to the heart!—Talk
not of hauling down your ensigns and standards when van-
quished—what is *that,* barber! to striking the flag that
Nature herself has nailed to the mast!''

Here noble Jack's feelings overcame him; he drooped
from the animated attitude into which his enthusiasm had
momentarily transported him; his proud head sunk upon
his chest . . . . [Pp. 360-361]

White-Jacket may try to justify Chase by saying that he bows
"to naval discipline afloat," even though he is "a stickler for
the Rights of Man, and the liberties of the world" when he is
on land (p. 17). But this is really a way for White-Jacket to
gloss over the fact that the system of the Neversink can un-
man even Chase. And one suspects that whether or not death
would have been the penalty for rescuing Ushant, Chase
might well have done little to help. He almost left White-
Jacket, one of his own, in the lurch, and death was surely not
the penalty for speaking up on that occasion.

Regardless, White-Jacket can never look on Chase as
mean or hypocritical; he needs too much what Chase can
most of the time provide for him. The structure of the Neversink makes everyone ineffectual; and, like Hamlet, Chase
compensates for his acquiescences with great amounts of
rhetoric and self-dramatization, all very attractive to the
men, because they themselves are in the same impotent state
that Jack is, including White-Jacket (would White-Jacket,
for example, really have killed Captain Claret, as he threatened
to do just before his arraignment at the mast, or is this just
a Chase-like pose in imitation of his hero?). Jack's talk gives
the men at least a champion of words and gestures, if not
deeds, someone swashbucklingly articulate. Chase can express their imprisoned fantasies of freedom. He is a poet and
legend-maker, who can quote Chaucer and Camoens, or

create a myth out of the ordinary facts of sea life, as when a shipmate, Shenly, is buried at sea, and Chase makes it an occasion for an allegory of the resurrection.

> "Look aloft," whispered Jack Chase. "See that bird! it is the spirit of Shenly."
> Gazing upward, all beheld a snow-white, solitary fowl, which . . . had been hovering over the main-mast during the service, and was now sailing far up into the depths of the sky. [P. 342]

Thus, even though Chase tends very much to be only the sum of the theatrics he indulges in, and would be powerless really to protect White-Jacket or to sustain the peace of the main-top if either were seriously threatened, White-Jacket treads very lightly and sentimentally on the subject of this man who he feels had "a heart in him like a mastodon's" (p. 320). It is not surprising that the book's final tableau is of White-Jacket, as usual, glorifying Chase.

> Hand in hand we top-mates stand, rocked in our Pisgah top. And over the starry waves, and broad out into the blandly blue and boundless night, . . . straight out into that fragrant night, ever-noble Jack Chase, matchless and unmatchable Jack Chase stretches forth his bannered hand, and, pointing shoreward, cries: "For the last time, hear Camoens, boys! . . . . " [P. 397]

Where, then, does all of this leave White-Jacket, and what is one to assume has been his progress toward the sort of relation to the world for which people like Judge Shaw, Peter Gansevoort, or Thomas Melville, Sr. were the models? In point of fact, the best Melville can do is to engage his narrator, and Chase, in an elaborate evasive action that seems only to reflect Melville's limited conception of male possibility for himself. It is significant, for example, that Melville chooses to place White-Jacket in an environment where he is at a disadvantage so great that retreat seems a perfectly justifiable mode of conduct. Melville appears to accept as a foregone conclsion that the world will always be too inimical to his protagonists to allow them to grow in the directions he felt pressured to take them. Thus, he can most easily relate to the egotism of Jack Chase, who against the unyielding realities of the Neversink sets his private world of romantic rhetoric, creating within it not only a haven for White-Jacket, but for himself also. This is the ultimate lesson White-Jacket learns from Chase: how to use language as a substitute for action, how to sermonize and philosophize—which he does in his narrative at the drop of a hat (indeed, most of the time while the hat is still tipping). But even White-Jacket's attacks on the Navy are from the seclusion of his writing-desk, after the fact; he leaves the work of *actual* reform to the public and to Congress. His role is hortatory, a role which is both self-gratifying, and eminently safe. White-Jacket, therefore, remains in the top, a satellite of Jack Chase, long after he leaves the Neversink.

White-Jacket, with the emotional predispositions toward egotism and withdrawal that seemed to be still very much intact in Melville's personality, foreshadows the appearance of *Moby-Dick* in the form it finally took:[8] a return to the self-indulgence characteristic of *Mardi.* Thus, it did not take much for Melville's reading of *Mosses from an Old Manse,* combined with his acquaintance with Hawthorne during 1850–1851, to precipitate in him once again an acute attack of Taji's old desire at the end of *Mardi* to be totally his "own soul's emperor" regardless of what the ordinary literary public might think of his behavior. Only this time Melville seemed to believe he could do it with more perfect tools than Taji had possessed. This time he seemed to feel he could create a piece of egotism that was so comprehensive that it might finally transcend any guilt, hostility, or insecurity he might feel about undertaking it. Taji had declined into over-compensation and suicidal depression because he could only imagine himself in futile opposition to what he conceived of as the world at large, a stage of self-regard at which all of Melville's first four narrators are frozen, and which, indeed, finally kills Ahab. But Ishmael's strategy is encirclement, not opposition; he wants to come to accept all things as equal parts of an indivisible totality where apparent contrarieties are resolved into extensions and complements of one another. Then, even if others could not accept the intellectual gyrings of the book as a reasonable basis for the conduct of life or authorship, Melville could accept them for himself without apology.

He wants to let his mind outrun the usually restrictive modes of human thought and emotion (including his own past modes), and take its shape from the example of the white whale. In the cetology chapters, the complexity and breadth of reference of the cetological facts implies that the whale is only a microcosmic reflection of the irreducible integrity of life as a whole; and Moby-Dick swims on, his back full of the iron flags that only signal the failure of anyone to ever limit him to their own conventional usages or preconceptions. For Melville, who was reaching at this time the explosive peak of his creative powers, and who was always at the mercy of some limiting financial or familial pressure, the white whale was an expression of his will to self-centered wholeness, to swimming on, no matter how punctured by what might be lethal darts to others. Melville sought to move before the face of his readers as the indestructible inhabitant of the whale-road of his own mind, free to graze in watery pastures miles deep, and to surface suddenly in air to the confusion of all who might seek to pursue him or to chart his mental course. As such, Melville was taking something of the same direction Emerson did, when, in trying to resolve the problem of freedom in a world where man seems everywhere hemmed in by fate, Emerson developed the strategy of training the mind to identify itself completely with the over-forces that run the universe. In this way, one becomes free by having his or her intellect become coextensive with the very system behind one's apparent enslavement.

> The day of days, the great day of the feast of life, is that in which the inward eye opens to the Unity in things, to the omnipresence of law:—sees that what is must be and ought to be, or is the best. This beatitude dips from on high down on us and we see. It is not in us so much as we are in it. If the air come to our lungs, we breathe and live; if not, we die. If the light come to our eyes, we see; else not. And if truth come to our mind we suddenly expand to its dimensions, as if we grew to worlds. We are as lawgivers; we speak for Nature; we prophesy and divine.[9]

And even in May of 1850, while *Moby-Dick* was still in its first, most unphilosophical stage of composition, untouched as yet by the influences of Hawthorne and his work, the general idea of whaleness was firmly associated in Melville's mind with the necessary process and shape of his new book.

> About the "whaling voyage"—I am half way in the work, & am very glad that your suggestion so jumps with mine. It will be a strange sort of a book, tho', I fear; blubber is blubber you know; tho' you may get oil out of it, the poetry runs as hard as sap from a frozen maple tree;— & to cook the thing up, one must needs throw in a little fancy, which from the nature of the thing, must be ungainly as the gambols of the whales themselves.[10]

Melville had therefore sensed all along that his most proper model of literary conduct must be leviathan, who can forever dispassionately cruise the immensities of its watery space, beyond the chronometrics of sailors and landlubbers both, bound only by some boundless sidereal imagination.

The major problem for Melville as it turned out, however, was that Ishmael never reaches that state of imagination, a state characterized, as Emerson was aware, by an all-consuming calm and "impersonality"[11]: creatures like the whale unselfconsciously pursue the life they feel so perfectly a part of. Ishmael remains only an initiant at this business, working hard and quite self-consciously to keep the latitude of his seas. While he is able, good naturedly, to encompass many points of view, there is still in him an unsatisfied hunger. The far-ranging complexity of his intelligence has, as yet, brought him no peace, although it shows the direction in which peace lies; at present, he is only magniloquently fumbling in that direction.

His incompleteness can be seen in his friendship with Queequeg. Queequeg is so attractive to Ishmael because he is, more than any other character in the book, the whale made human, leviathan as chummy.[12] Significantly, however, Ishmael winds up using Queequeg only partly as a model for his own independent conduct; he also uses Queequeg as a presence on which he can rely to be a center of safety for him—much like Jack Chase and Chase's main-top. Melville had for so long been convinced that his narrators, and himself, would always need something or someone in addition to themselves to produce the sense of security they always craved, that he cannot portray full self-assurance even in his most grandly egotistical *persona*. Thus, while *Moby-Dick* is, in many ways, a very highly evolved expression of confidence and strength, the child in both Ishmael and Melville still could not at bottom believe that he could become his own best hope of survival by himself.

Queequeg is, indeed, a figure of enormous psychological stability compared to Ishmael. He need not go through the discursive mental gymnastics Ishmael does, because he already possesses the integration of personality Ishmael can only hope for. Ishmael's mind must keep moving, because to stop moving would be to leave himself open and unguarded. Thus, there is always a hint of the frantic in his constant compulsion to verbalize. Queequeg's tranquility, on the other hand, comes from the fact that his mind is stationary and utterly self-possessed. So, he can accept being the Prince of Kokovoko or a harpooneer aboard the Pequod with the same equanimity. Even the tattoos he carries on his body—tattoos that Ishmael feels would unriddle the universe if they could be read properly—are only frustrating to others, not to Queequeg.

> Many spare hours [Queequeg] spent, in carving the lid [of his coffin] with all manner of grotesque figures and drawings; and it seemed that hereby he was striving, in his rude way, to copy parts of the twisted tattooing on his body. And this tattooing, had been the work of a departed prophet and seer of his island, who, by those hieroglyphic marks, had written out on his body a complete theory of the heavens and the earth, and a mystical treatise on the art of attaining truth; so that Queequeg in his own proper person was a riddle to unfold; a wondrous work in one volume; but whose mysteries not even himself could read though his own live heart beat against them; and these mysteries were therefore destined . . . to . . . be unsolved to the last. And this thought it must have been which suggested to Ahab that wild exclamation of his, when one morning turning away from surveying poor Queequeg—"Oh, devilish tantalization of the gods!" [P. 399][13]

Queequeg, of course, has no need to "read" the "wondrous work" he himself is. He lives in unreflective harmony with his mysteries because they are part of the texture of his muscles and tissues, his whole being. His mind does not have to solve the riddles first, and then communicate these solutions to his body, making the body respond to the intellectual synthesis. And so, Ishmael talks a great deal, while Queequeg talks hardly at all.

One effect of Queequeg's composure that is particularly attractive to the insecure side of Ishmael's personality is that Queequeg possesses a constancy of physical commitment to other human beings, Ishmael most especially. In chapter 10, he tells Ishmael that "he would gladly die for [him], if need should be" (p. 53); and in chapter 12, Ishmael relates that Queequeg "at once resolved to accompany me to [Nantucket], ship aboard the same vessel, get into the same watch, the same boat, the same mess with me, in short to share my every hap; with both my hands in his, boldly dip into the Potluck of both worlds" (p. 57). Indeed, Queequeg is loyal and protective even in death; when the coffin he had prepared for himself saves Ishmael, it is clear that whatever was the force of personality that gave Queequeg his psychological and physical strength, it is such a potent spiritual commodity that even after the death of Queequeg's body, it can perpetuate itself and keep the promises that the body could not. Ishmael becomes aware of this energy in chapter 110, when Queequeg is first working on his coffin; Ishmael glimpses a strength in him that seems to expand to the bounds of eternity.

> But as all else in him thinned, . . . his eyes, nevertheless, seemed growing fuller and fuller; they became of a strange softness of lustre; and mildly but deeply looked out at you there from his sickness, a wondrous testimony to that immortal health in him which could not die, or be weakened. And like circles on the water, which, as they grow fainter, expand; so his eyes seemed rounding and rounding, like the rings of Eternity. An awe that cannot be named would steal over you as you sat by the side of this waning savage, and saw . . . strange things in his face . . . . [Pp. 395-396]

Of course, Ishmael had received the ministrations of Queequeg's awesome personality as early as the famous passage in chapter 10 where a sense of emotional reconciliation with a world he has obviously been alienated from for some time is temporarily restored to Ishmael.

> . . . I began to be sensible of strange feelings. I felt a melting in me. No more my splintered heart and maddened hand were turned against the wolfish world. This soothing savage had redeemed it. There he sat, his very indifference speaking a nature in which there lurked no civilized hypocrisies and bland deceits. [P. 53]

Queequeg's calm creates calm in the narrator; his soundness generates harmony similar to that which Ishmael feels in the center of the whale herd in chapter 87: "[W]e glided between two whales into the innermost heart of the shoal, as if from some mountain torrent we had slid into a serene valley lake" (p. 324). Interestingly, the geography of this simile is the same as the geography of Nukuheva; amidst the whales, Ishmael experiences the sort of tranquility Tommo often felt in Typee Valley, where the natives lived in complete integration of themselves with their surroundings. "Amid the tornadoed Atlantic of my being, do I myself still for ever centrally disport in mute calm; and while ponderous planets of unwaning woe revolve round me, deep down and deep inland there I still bathe me in eternal mildness of joy" (p. 326). It is "inland," also, that Ishmael is carried in the vision he has while squeezing sperm, a vision which is for him an emotional epiphany: "[A]s I snuffed up that uncontaminated aroma,—literally and truly, like the smell of spring violets; I declare to you, that for the time I lived as in a musky meadow . . . ." (p. 348). And just as Mehevi welcomed Tommo into Typee Valley, Queequeg, too, is chief over an inland calm he carries within himself, into which he welcomes the voyaging white man.

Still, the relationship between them is only "momentarily, incompletely, and ambiguously successful";[14] and Ahab gradually comes to replace Queequeg as the focus of Ishmael's attention, a replacement that is only further evidence of Melville's uncertainties about his narrator's strengths, and Ishmael's uncertainties about himself. There is no way for Ishmael, on his own, to truly match Queequeg's personality and become his equal. He never develops the emotional composure to fully meet Queequeg on the ground of Queeque's own calm, loving constancy. He is too distracted by other things, too self-conscious, too little like a whale to swim for very long with those who are. Whatever coming together may be briefly possible in a snug bed on Nantucket, therefore, is not the general order of Ishmael and Queequeg's relationship. Even the monkey-rope incident in chapter 72, which at first appears to dramatize the perpetuation of their deep emotional bond, really demonstrates just the reverse. Ishmael would prefer to

> get rid of the dangerous liabilities which the [monkey-rope] entailed.
>
> So strongly and metaphysically did I conceive of my situation then, that . . . I seemed distinctly to perceive that my own individuality was now merged in a joint stock company of two; that my free will had received a mortal wound; and that another's mistake or misfortune might plunge innocent me into unmerited disaster and death. Therefore, I saw that here was a sort of interregnum in Providence; for its even-handed equity never could have sanctioned so gross an injustice. And yet still further pondering—while I jerked him now and then from between the whale and the ship, . . . I saw that this situation of mine was the precise situation of every mortal that breathes; only, in most cases, he, one way or other, has this Siamese connexion with a plurality of other mortals. [P. 271]

There is little enthusiasm here for Ishmael's own "Siamese connexion." He may snatch some cold comfort from his recognition that all men are in the same position as himself, but it is neither philosophically nor emotionally satisfying. Indeed, his emphasis is more on himself as a victim than on anything else. Thus, no matter how hard Ishmael may strive toward a liberation from his own insecurities, he will never lose his sense of vulnerability; and this troubles him, even to the point of resenting Queequeg for his unknowing part in a circumstance that reminds him how tenuous a hold he actually has on any kind of self-assurance.

When Ahab comes on the scene, he quintessentially expresses that prison of mystery and uncertainty within which Ishmael is inevitably caught. Queequeg, from his alien way of life, will never have to be concerned with this burden. Whatever Ishmael's desire, therefore, to be like the whale or like Queequeg, the truth is that Ahab is what Ishmael instinctively knows he might more easily become. So it is Ahab with whom Ishmael finally feels the strongest relation. For example, when Ishmael ostensibly plays the genial polymath and foil to Ahab's monomania, Ishmael is as much a figure of antisocial behavior as Ahab. As Edwin Miller has recognized, Ishmael's verbal reductionism—his constant habit of cutting the legs out from under people and ideas—places him in much the same position that Ahab occupies.

> The reductionism . . . enables Ishmael to mask his "tornadoed" feelings and his alienation. The wit, often aggressive and hostile, is encased in a socially acceptable form. Ishmael does not knock off hats literally, but wittily. With impunity he punishes the world that has punished him. Like Ahab he takes his vengeance. Both are frightened boy-men. If Ahab is "unbuttoned" and assumes a quixotic kind of heroism, Ishmael's comedy not only "unbuttons" the whale but the readers and himself. A contemporary reviewer in *The Literary World* in November 1851 speaks, perceptively, of "Ishmael, whose wit may be allowed to be against everything on land, as his hand is against everything at sea." His verbal aggression undermines orthodoxy, philosophy, mythology, and human aspiration.[15]

It is good to note also that Ishmael's violence is not always confined to purely rhetorical manifestations. Ishmael, while he seeks the whale primarily to know it and imitate it, regularly participates in the murder of the very creatures he is always so ready to eulogize. There seems to be a portion of his personality quite willing to take advantage of the socially acceptable enterprise of whaling to express its own bloody desire, like Ahab's, for dominance rather than intellectual interpenetration. This is why Ishmael is so readily caught up in Ahab's demented ceremony with the harpoons in chapter 36, and it is also why there is an essential contradiction in Ishmael's epiphany while squeezing sperm in chapter 94: the substance that marvellously creates for him a kind of emotional pastorale comes from the whale he has just had a hand in slaughtering.

Lastly, Ahab and Ishmael share the mutual condition of being sea-orphans. We are not given all the details about Ahab, but some fate he is under and which he loathes (though he cannot alter it) has driven him from the green and tranquil land on which he was raised, out to make war on the sea. He cannot even remember why; perhaps he never knew. On a beautiful clear day, Ahab, age eighteen, kills his first whale; and then he finds he must play out for the rest of his life the hand he did not even know he was being dealt until he turned to see the cards already laid out before him. He says to Starbuck in chapter 132:

> When I think of this life I have led; the desolation of solitude it has been; the masoned, walled-town of a Captain's exclusiveness, which admits but small entrance to any sympathy from the green country without . . . when I think of all this; only half-suspected, not so keenly known to me before—and how for forty years I have fed upon dry salted fare—fit emblem of the dry nourishment of my soul!—when the poorest landsman has had fresh fruit to his daily hand, and broken the world's fresh bread, to my mouldy crusts . . . . I feel deadly faint, bowed, and humped, as though I were Adam [the original outcast son, driven from the safety of his Father's garden], staggering beneath the piled centures since Paradise. [Pp. 443-444]

This sense of alienation and incompleteness that dominates Ahab's destructive emotions is the same that perpetually drives Ishmael's expansiveness. For Melville, Ahab and Ishmael are inescapably twinned, a recognition that Ishmael, in his constant fascination with Ahab, shares. It also shows in Ishmael's final loneliness, which comes from more than his being the last survivor of the Pequod's sinking. Ishmael was striving toward a condition of personality that could move among the most dangerous contradictions of life with some skill, and without losing its humanity, as Ahab came to do. But when at last he seems most conclusively free of Ahab's monomania and the doomed ship it was driving toward destruction, Ishmael also seems most desolate. He did not want to lose Ahab; Ahab expressed part of himself that was very real for him, even when he knew that it was narrow-minded and antilife. At the same time, he wanted to imitate Queequeg, but could finally never have the confidence necessary to complete the task alone. And so Ishmael, neither Ahab nor Queequeg, neither shark nor whale, is left to drift disappointedly on an open sea. Whatever gracefully self-sustaining image Melville started out in *Moby-Dick* to construct for Ishmael, by the end he has returned to the lasting desolation so much a part of his every expression of himself. Always, "it's a long stage, and no inn in sight, and night coming, and the body cold."[16]

Perhaps only the lost father can provide the necessary warmth; but as Ishmael sees, "the secret of our paternity lies in [the] grave, and we must there to learn it" (p. 406). Perhaps, after all, the death of Ahab was a blessing, not a defeat; perhaps that sailor, at least, found final succor somewhere. Death, too, might have been a blessing for Ishmael. For the lost boy, survival, not extinction, is the curse.

Notes

1. Hugh W. Hetherington, *Melville's Reviewers* (Chapel Hill: University of North Carolina Press, 1961), p. 128.

2. Letter of 5 June 1849, in Merrell R. Davis and William H. Gilman, eds., *The Letters of Herman Melville* (New Haven: Yale University Press, 1960), p. 86.

3. Letter of 6 October 1849, ibid., pp. 91-92.

4. Letter of 5 June 1849, ibid., p. 86.

5. Harrison Hayford, Hershel Parker, and G. Thomas Tanselle, eds., *Redburn,* (Evanston and Chicago: Northwestern University Press and the Newberry Library, 1969).

6. The flyleaves of the guidebook show the extensiveness of the father's finances, cultural interests, and social connections (p. 144).

7. Harrison Hayford, Hershel Parker, and G. Thomas Tanselle, eds., *White-Jacket,* (Northwestern University Press and the Newberry Library, 1970).

8. For the stages of the book's composition, see Howard P. Vincent, *The Trying-Out of Moby-Dick* (Boston: Houghton, Mifflin Co., 1949), pp. 13-52.

9. Stephen E. Whicher, ed., "Fate," in *Selections from Ralph Waldo Emerson* (Boston: Houghton, Mifflin Co., 1957), p. 341.

10. Letter to Richard Henry Dana, 1 May 1850, in Davis and Gilman, p. 108.

11. "Fate," in *Selections,* p. 341.

12. I would differ with Robert Zoellner in my assigning of symbols to Queequeg's personality. See Mr. Zoellner's *The Salt-Sea Mastodon* (Berkeley: University of California Press, 1973), pp. 215-238.

13. Harrison Hayford and Hershel Parker, eds., *Moby-Dick* (New York: W. W. Norton and Co., 1967).

14. Paul Brodtkorb, *Ishamel's White World* (New Haven: Yale University Press, 1965), p. 55.

15. Edwin Miller, *Melville* (New York: George Braziller, 1975), p. 218.

16. Letter to Hawthorne, 17 November 1851, in Davis and Gilman, p. 143.

5

Pierre and After

HAWTHORNE'S removal in 1851 from Lenox, and from Melville's immediate sphere of acquaintance, not only seems to have determined the antifeminine direction of *Pierre,*it also seems to have been the principal cause of *Pierre's* becoming Melville's most undisguised expression of self-hatred. *Pierre* suggests, in more than just its renewed anxiety over women, that, with Hawthorne gone, Melville was struggling to keep from drowning underneath that feeling of helplessness that was never very far away from his personality, even in the best of circumstances. He apparently needed, and quickly, some way to patch up his failing hopes for a continuance of the large, superior egotism that he had tried to make dominate *Moby-Dick*. Feeling much less genial than Ishmael, however, he turned to the consciously vicious annihilation of Pierre, the representative of that insecure, childlike part of himself that had allowed him to become far more dependent on his friendship with Hawthorne than was good for him; and the cruelty Melville displays toward his young protagonist shows the literary extremity to which he felt he had to go in order to salvage, alone, any vestiges of the self-confidence he had let himself experience while Hawthorne was close by. In *Pierre* Melville is more conscious than ever before that the lost boy he forever carried within him not only got in the way of accepting the other-directed ethos of the Melville and Gansevoort patriarchs, but was also capable of keeping him from undertaking any fully realized exercise of the personality he had begun developing in *Moby-Dick* as an alternative to that ethos.

Therefore, in destroying Pierre, Melville made a desperate attempt to hold on to some of the psychological ground he felt he had gained with Ishmael. Especially through the device of himself as omniscient, intrusive narrator in *Pierre,* Melville can project an image of his own more comprehensive intelligence as compared to his protagonist's painful naïveté and imperfectly controlled vulnerability. But the murderous ascendency Melville gains over Pierre showed, by its very murderousness, that Melville was fighting a rearguard emotional action. *Pierre* stood no real chance of freeing Melville from his mental trammels, and was, in fact, the beginning of his decline into not only literary and personal obscurity, but the misanthropy so consummately embodied in a work like *The Confidence-Man.* As things turned out, it was not until *Billy Budd* that Melville was able to neutralize the conflict that the writing of *Pierre* so epitomized. By the late 1880s he had arrived at a stage of consciousness where he could live without any sort of self-hatred, and where he felt no temptations to egotistical rebellion against the idea of involvement in an ordinary, day-to-day life of masculine responsibilities. The result was that *Billy Budd,* more successfully than any previous work, accepted the necessity of those responsibilities, and at the same time dealt in a detached and benevolent way with what Melville could only handle with such contumely in *Pierre*—his ambivalent desire for the secure innocence of a life without knowledge, for the insular, prelapsarian world of his early youth.

When he first completed *Moby-Dick,* it was certainly true that he did not feel any of the despair that would so shortly come to drive the composition of *Pierre.* Indeed, for a brief while Melville was able to imagine that *Moby-Dick* opened entirely new possibilities for him, and that it had helped to purge him of some of his perpetual spleen. He could even feel that the whale was only the beginning of the powerful avatars he could develop for himself: "So, now, let us add Moby Dick to our blessing, and step from that. Leviathan is not the biggest fish;—I have heard of Krakens."[1] The perpetuation of these feelings, however, seems to have been largely contingent upon Hawthorne's reinforcement of them. Melville might assert to Hawthorne that "a sense of unspeakable security is in me [about *Moby-Dick*]"; but this is only "on account of [Hawthorne's] having understood the book."[2] Melville places himself in the same position of dependence with Hawthorne that White-Jacket did with Chase, his literary master. But the dangers of Melville's dependence are much greater and more susceptible to disappointment because Melville, in addition, appears to have been projecting onto Hawthorne an appreciation of *Moby-Dick* that Hawthorne either did not possess, or only marginally displayed. For example, there is a distinctly hectic luster in Melville's description to Hawthorne of how he reacted to Hawthorne's letter (now lost) about *Moby-Dick*.

Whence come you, Hawthorne? By what right do you drink from my flagon of life? And when I put it to my lips—lo, they are yours and not mine. I feel that the Godhead is broken up like the bread at the Supper, and that we are the pieces. Hence this infinite fraternity of feeling. Now, sympathizing with the paper, my angel turns over another page. You did not care a penny for the book. But, now and then as you read, you understood the pervading thought that impelled the book—and that you praised. Was it not so? You were archangel enough to despise the imperfect body, and embrace the soul . . . .

. . . . Farewell. Don't write a word about the book. That would be robbing me of my miserly delight. I am heartily sorry I ever wrote anything about you—it was paltry.[3]

One senses here that Melville's whole mental life, along with his confidence in his capacities as an artist, hangs from the very insubstantial thread of what Melville can *make himself believe* Hawthorne believed about *Moby-Dick*. Melville could accept the apparently indeterminate appreciation contained in Hawthorne's "letter, which, without citing any particular examples, yet intimated the part-&-parcel allegoricalness of the whole,"[4] as a ground he felt was substantial to stand on in relation to his work and his future. He could make himself believe that Hawthorne was giving the great seal of artistic approval to his most self-centered work, and so was washing away forever any conflict Melville need feel about conforming to his family's traditions of behavior. Hawthorne's gentle nature did not seem at all prone to disabusing Melville of this image of his support; and Melville could rest contented in the fact that the man he imagined loved him and understood him best remained near him.

But once Hawthorne left, whatever rest, whatever catharsis *Moby-Dick* had promised, evaporated; only a few months after seeing "The Whale" through the presses, Melville had locked himself away to furiously scribble on *Pierre*. Friends, in fact, feared for his health, in particular his neighbor, Sarah Morewood, who, in December of 1851, recounted that she had "laughed at [Melville] somewhat and told him that the recluse life he was leading made his city friends think he was slightly insane—he replied that long ago he came to the same conclusion himself but that if he left home to look after Hungary the cause in hungery would suffer . . . ."[5] Melville may here put Mrs. Morewood off with a pleasant pun, playing the role of potboiler novelist, making believe that his only concern is selling books so no one will have to go hungry; but his saddened humor does not even begin to tell the tale of what motivates him. After all, he was working on a book he must have known no one would buy: in fact, he was parodying the very sort of work that would have sold, and then complicating the matter by turning the parody gradually into a piece of tortured psychosexual melodrama. He was certainly serving no cause in "hungery" by that sort of writing. Nor was he expanding the scope of his previous efforts by such outrageous literary behavior—*Pierre* is a much smaller and more bitter work than *Moby-Dick*. If Melville had imagined krakens to be his next pursuit, he wound up only shooting fish in a barrel with his history of the pathetic and pitiful decline of the heir to Saddle Meadows. What cause, then, was Melville really serving? Perhaps that of the very sanity he seemed to outsiders so to be jeopardizing. In murdering Pierre, as has been noted, he wanted to strangle his own foolish insecurities: the things that had caused him to hurl so much of himself into his relations with Hawthorne, only to have the friendship disappear; the things that were at the root of the ever-present desperation that dogged his literary efforts, never allowing him to rest his pen from telling over and over the same story, which always had the same frustrating conclusion for his homeless sailors, even in *Moby-Dick*. Was he not, at the end of 1851, still the same too tender-hearted individual as always, whatever *persona* he might wish to show to the world; and would he not be hurt again and again, by every other Hawthorne, or Mehevi, or Harry Bolton, or Allan Melville that came into his life, and to whom he would hang on like death? It must have seemed to Melville that all this had to stop somewhere; so he tried to make *Pierre* the point of no return, the point where he might prove without question that he was above his own so-evident confusions.

Pierre's fall is designed from the beginning with blood in Melville's eye. If there is a single character in his fiction that he seems to want crushed without mercy, it is Pierre. For example, the insular and safe Saddle Meadows Melville creates as the beloved environment of his protagonist's youth is deliberately made very fragile. Then Melville smashes this environment to bits right in front of Pierre, throwing him out of the garden of his best hopes, and into situations that, by the end, grind him down to nothing. Indeed, no matter how bad Melville makes things for Pierre, he seems always to pursue him one step further, to strike him again and again. In the end, when Pierre has lost almost everything, and is living a life beyond hope of repair or meaning, Melville still introduces the climaxing ambiguity of the picture in the New York gallery that impels Pierre on to the final embrace of death. It is clear that Melville plans to leave Pierre with nothing—no family, no father, no honor, no love, no achievement. He gives Pierre over to drunkenness, comatose seizures, and despair, creating a protagonist who winds up wandering around falling down in the gutters. He does not even get to keep his life, miserable as it is.

Only Melville is left alive, the teller of the tale. Melville uses his own voice to recount Pierre's story, speaking to his reader without any intermediating *persona;* and by reducing Pierre to a lump of foolishly mortal clay, Melville, as narrator, demands recognition of his own wholeness, his own transcendence of Pierre's hopeless condition, urging upon both his readers and himself the idea of the superiority of his own mind compared to that of his protagonist. Thus, in passage after passage where he analyzes Pierre's psychological situation, Melville shows that he can himself articulate things Pierre has not even begun to learn yet. Melville's voice is never willing to simplify or palliate—his function is to tell the whole truth as far as it can be known. "But I shall follow the endless, winding way,—the flowing river in the cave of man; careless whither I be led, reckless where I land" (p. 107).[6] There are in Pierre's story "mysteries interpierced with mysteries, and mysteries eluding mysteries" (p. 142), but Melville feels he can successfully thread the labyrinthine maze of human motivation and circumstance that so confounds Pierre. Thus, as Melville works his way around an increasingly complex set of phenomena, he, unlike Pierre, always seems able to hold the complexities in suspension and never be overwhelmed by them. He is very anxious to display this detached superiority right from the beginning; already in Book 1, chapter 2, Melville is looking far ahead to Pierre's decline, and asserting his own more comprehensive insight: "Pierre little foresaw that this world hath a secret deeper than beauty, and Life some burdens heavier than death" (p. 7). Two brief chapters later, one can almost feel Melville gloating over what he has in store for Pierre, things which Melville most confidently understands, but which he will have to teach Pierre the hard way:

> So [Saddle Meadows] was a glorious benediction to young Pierre; we shall see if that blessing pass from him as did the divine blessing from the Hebrews; we shall yet see again, I say, whether Fate hath not just a little bit of a word or two to say in this world; we shall see whether this wee scrap of latinity be very far out of the way—*Nemo contra Deum nisi Deus ipse.* [P. 14]

There is just the edge of a tone of condescension here, a tone that often breaks out into "choked and terrible staccato laughter."[7]

> It is not until the last third of Book Two that [this] tone relents at all. And even then, until the end of the novel, the tone seldom entirely loses its edge of distaste and sarcasm .... for the tone always works hard to enable the narrator to show the reader that Pierre's goal is pathetically hopeless and foolish and murderous.[8]

While Melville is very conscious of Pierre's mother and father, and Isabel all as agents of Pierre's downfall, still Melville hates and blames Pierre himself, hates and blames that sort of personality that has no way of adequately evaluating its experiences, and so makes its life a series of unproven fears, naive misunderstandings, and misleading projections. Melville finally (if unreasonably) holds Pierre responsible for himself—only in that way can Melville justify his own cruelty toward him.

Melville, therefore, ostensibly playing the part of detached narrator, is not detached at all; if he were, there would be no need for him to treat Pierre's decline as unpleasantly as he does. In trying to force his own emotional life to an impossible climax, Melville was only, in fact, demonstrating how far away he was from coming to any meaningful terms with his feelings. One senses this, too, in his attempts during 1852 to interest the absent Hawthorne in writing the "Agatha" story, the details of which Melville had picked up on a trip to Nantucket.[9] Regardless of all the anger at his own weaknesses in *Pierre,* Melville could not resist a final wooing of Hawthorne's favor. Although their relationship was clearly over, Melville tried vainly to establish some rapprochement on the pretext of providing Hawthorne with grist for his literary mill. Hawthorne, however, courteously but fimly declined Melville's offers and the covert expressions of need they embodied, even when Melville went so far as to visit him personally at Concord about the matter of the story in November of 1852. Thus, Hawthorne was still unalterably lost to Melville, and *Pierre* had obviously not done its work of making Melville an independent creature. He was back, as he always was, to where he had started: alone, with prospects more darkly closed down than ever before.

In consequence, Melville's literary career between *Pierre* and *The Confidence-Man* shows a loss of spirit, a sense of having nowhere to go. The limbo Melville's work passed into is apparent in a number of things, but two particularly. To begin with, except for *The Confidence-Man*, his work during this period is piecemeal. For the first time, he turns to magazine fiction, and even to a serialized novel, *Israel Potter*. He seems to have lost whatever it was that impelled the long, sustained works he had been doing. Yet Melville was unable to break old habits. In 1854, for example, "when Elizabeth and the children went to Boston on their annual Thanksgiving visit, accordingly, Herman went with them. They missed the train on the morning of Tuesday, November 26, and he had an extra day in his upstairs study—where he went 'as usual,' according to his mother. But he had no urgent business there.''[10] Melville gladly returned to the one place that had great meaning for him; but now his imagintion and emotions could not be pressed to the kinds of efforts that had been so much a part of his life for eight years. He had exhausted and voided himself with the enmities of *Pierre;* it was impossible for him to make any new beginnings. To argue, therefore, that Melville turned to magazines in order to guarantee some steady income or to recoup some popularity, or to give himself a rest, does not seem to tell the whole story. Melville had bucked public taste before; he had worked to exhaustion before. So, to go into a prolonged period of small labors argues that Melville no longer had the psychological stakes to put up; the game had finally gotten beyond him.

The second thing that impresses one about this period is the recurrence, with predictable regularity, of stories that have to do with individuals whose lives are winding down to an obscure death. Thus, while stories like "The Happy Failure," "The Lightning-Rod Man," "The Fiddler," and Hunilla's sketch in "The Encantadas" all seem to affirm the individual's ability to face with some dignity forces that try to coerce or destroy him, on the whole the affirmative note in the short fiction is very weak. It is true that Melville was, during this time, trying to work out some attitude toward what Leon Howard has called "nonaggresive but unshakable patience,"[11] which was one of the things that seemed to interest Melville in the "Agatha" story. But if Melville could no longer sustain works like *Moby-Dick* where he pitted the heroic dementia of Ahab against the adventurous deep-sightedness of Ishmael, neither could he, finally, reach toward patience as the placebo for his turmoil. While he might see it abstractly as a great virtue, it was not a virtue to which Melville's restless personality could form any real attachment. In those works dealing with patience, in fact, Melville resists long-suffering submission as a solution to problems. His patient figures are mostly victims, or, as John Seelye has remarked, prisoners.[12] In the post-*Pierre* fiction, they are no better off than Melville's previous aggressors. Benito Cereno is as empty as the skeleton on the front of his ship; Bartleby dies curled up in front of a wall in the Tombs, having affirmed nothing but his lack of affirmation; Jimmy Rose becomes a ragged spectre who haunts the tea times of his old acquaintances. Even Hunilla, beatified by Melville because she embodies humanity's great capacity to endure, has her story wedged between two of the most discouraging sketches in "The Encantadas"—that of Charles's Island, with its Dog-King, and that of the despicable hermit, Oberlus. Hunilla's tale, like the grave of the sailor that is "found in a bleak gorge of Chatham Isle," is "tucked in with clinkers."[13] When Melville derives any chilly comfort from her life, it is quite brief, and not unalloyed with despair.

This imagination of disaster bore its final fruit in 1857, with the publication of *The Confidence-Man:*

> Wearied and exasperated by the relentless underlying conflict and confounded by the constant inversions of value from positive to negative and negative to positive, [a] man may finally arrive at a stage of virtual paralysis with no capacity for decision, one effect of which is the apprehension that everything is almost equally meaningless and worthless . . . .[14]

The central character of *The Confidence-Man* fabricates his own conflicts with others as a series of tricks or jokes, and so vitiates, in the very creation of them, any meaning they could possibly have. *The Confidence-Man* is a novel, which, however odd it may seem, does not really exist. It is, in its own eccentric way, Melville's most brilliant creation, and at the same time, no creation at all, an attempt at an ultimte expression of Emily Dickinson's sense of "Zero at the Bone."[15] "The nihilism with which [Melville] had toyed for so long spreads like an ague through the fibers of his art during the period following *Pierre,* and, with the writing of *The Confidence-Man,* all activity ceases, with character and style solidifying into a perfect cipher of ambiguity."[16] One is left nothing to cling to as a reality in the book, and it becomes a novel that "seems to invalidate the possibility of meaningful fiction."[17] As it finally turned out, therefore, *Pierre,* rather than being the testament of Melville's emotional independence, as his authorial voice would have liked his audience to believe, turned out to be the first line of Melville's epitaph as a writer of fiction. The crisis of its composition brought forth not new directions, but rather nondirections; after *The Confidence-Man,* Melville did not write any fiction for over thirty years.

When he began again, late in the 1880s, with *Billy Budd,* he had reached a stage in his life where, it seems, he could negotiate a better arrangement with his emotions than previously. He was in circumstances that did not demand he be anything but what he was—an old man passing on toward death—and there was freedom in this. For once in his life, Melville did not have to worry about money; he had as much as he required from bequests made by expiring relatives. Nor was he subject to family pressures: most of his family had disappeared into memories. All of his aunts and uncles, along with his father-in-law, were dead, as were his mother, and all his brothers and sisters except Catherine. His own two sons were dead. His daughter Frances was married, which left only Elizabeth and Bessie (his youngest daughter) around the house. These losses, of course, created some quite depressing times for him, but they also released him at last from that net of family obligations and imperatives in which he had always felt bound. Certainly his relations with Lizzie had become significantly more tender. She, and perhaps women generally, had ceased to represent any threat to him, and, at his death, he was even in the final stages of putting together a volume of poems assembled specifically for her.

This is not to say that Melville had undergone some com-

plete revolution of outlook; the scar tissue from ancient
wounds accumulated over the six decades since his father's
death would always give him cause for some sadness and bitterness. This was partly why, in *Billy Budd,* he returns to a
variation of the killing ground of *Pierre*—the orphan innocent, now in the shape of Billy Budd, must die. If he is allowed
to live, he may drag all around him down with him. The difference, however, in *Billy Budd* is that Billy is killed off by
Melville so that Melville can provide him with eternal reward,
not ugly damnation. In fact, in the way he has Billy die,
Melville even preseves his innocence, and provides him with
an apotheosis—a far cry from the killing of Pierre, where
Melville felt it requisite to denigrate Pierre utterly before doing him in. Through the glorious death he hands Billy,
Melville is able to make an act of faith that innocence will
receive its proper desert in some future life even if in this life
it is only a source of potential pain and confusion. Thus, a
major part of *Billy Budd's* function in Melville's canon, and
in the pattern of Melville's psychology, is to provide him with
a literary form for making that faith credible, a form that
allows an act of belief from Melville's heart in the ultimate
justification of innocence.

His portrayal of Vere, on the other hand, allowed Melville
to express two further reconciliations with himself. First of
all, Melville demonstrated, through the respect he allows
Vere to command, a quieting of the impulses in himself
toward both childish dependency, and egotistic rebellion as a
compensation for guilt over that dependency. Melville shows
a great willingness to accept the idea of stable, externally
oriented male behavior that Vere represents as more important for life than any sort of withdrawal or indulgence.
Melville has Vere gain stature in the reader's eyes precisely
because he is not like Taji, Ahab, or Ishamel. Secondly, the
use of Vere made possible for Melville a final act of
forgiveness of the world's betrayals. Vere takes a paternal interest in Billy, the sailor-orphan; and, in the confrontation

with Claggart, it is Vere's responsibility either to preserve intact the safety of Billy's innocent world, or to fracture it, just as, sixty years before, Allan Melville had held a similar responsibility with respect to Herman's world. It is true that Vere chooses the latter course, and in so doing partly follows the pattern of all those people and things in Melville that seemed always to promise safety to his protagonists, but that in the end were agents of painful ambiguity: Typee Valley, Saddle Meadows, Walter Redburn's guidebook, Harry Bolton, Yillah. Yet *Billy Budd,* in its treatment of Vere, reconciles itself to the idea of betrayal with more true equanimity than anything before it. Vere, caught among the simultaneous and confusing demands made on him by such things as Claggart's evil, Billy's innocence, the Nore Mutiny, his own sense of justice, and the Articles of War, tries to maintain a sense of proper proportion. It may not be perfect, and its emotional consequences may, at times, be unhappy ones, but Melville does not fault Vere's attempt. He feels no need to react with feelings of blight or desolation against what Vere stands for. Melville had at least come to accept the *necessity* of what Vere does; he could excuse it on that ground and even commiserate with Vere for having to do it. In *Billy Budd,* therefore, Melville takes the world as it is, but populates it with figures like Billy and Vere, whom he does not feel compelled to embarrass. This in no way implies that Melville was simplifying things, or that he was becoming overly sanguine about man's perpetual bout with existence. Melville could no more be a bearer of pie-in-the-sky optimism in 1890 than he could in 1857. What he did was to admit finally that faith and unostentatious, realistic-minded struggle had some importance in an ever-ambiguous and dangerous world.

Melville's act of faith is most graphically shown in Billy's hanging, because Billy's death opens a new life for him that transcends restriction or pain. On the verge of this new life, he pronounces his famous benediction, " 'God bless Captain

Vere!' . . . . syllables . . . delivered in the clear melody of a singing bird on the point of launching from the twig'' (p. 123.)[18] With his last words, Billy ascends to a place beyond the hopes of any of Melville's previous characters.

> . . . it chanced that the vapory fleece hanging low in the East was shot through with a soft glory as of the fleece of the Lamb of God seen in mystical vision, and simultaneously therewith, watched by the wedged mass of upturned faces, Billy ascended; and, ascending, took the full rose of the dawn. [P. 124]

This is a transfiguration of all of Melville's settings of peace and safety into a final, inviolable landscape. The "soft glory" of the fleece is divine, and the rose, both as color and as image for the blossoming presence of dawn, is the "full" one of universal rebirth. Melville demonstrates his allegiance to a vision of an innocence that can finally achieve embodiment in something greater than the world or the individual psyche. He appears to accept traditional Christian theology in this regard. He is at least accepting certain of Christianity's symbols to represent his own best hopes and feelings.

To enable his last work of fiction to express this belief in the ultimate triumph of innocence, Melville preserves Billy in a particularly simple psychological and moral state. The key word here is "preserve," for Melville deliberately organizes Billy's life not only so that he must die but also so that he remains innocent. To begin with, Melville keeps Billy from any sustained engagement in the darker areas of human perception until he is confronted by Claggart in the presence of Vere. Consider, for instance, that even though Billy is an orphan, his separation from his parents occurred so early that he could not even have remembered it. He has not undergone the sense of blight people like Pierre and Redburn do. And unlike Isabel—also deprived of her birthright—his life has not served as a constantly rankling reminder of loss. In fact, the position he enjoys among his shipmates, and the carefree existence he has had at sea, produce just the opposite effect. Even when Billy, after Claggart's accusation, appears to conform to the Melvillean pattern of the frustrated innocent turned destroyer, the victim is not a guiltless bystander, such as Isabel, Lucy or Starbuck. Melville makes Claggart an allegory of Satan, a figure of the most deceitful kind of evil; and so Billy, by striking him down, is not plunged into the moral abyss of victim become victimizer that Melville opened beneath Pierre and Ahab.

Melville also uses the device of compression of time to preserve Billy's innocence. Billy is never unavoidably faced with the world's black underside until he encounters Claggart;and it is also not until he strikes Claggart that Billy comes to understand that true justice and man's justice are not the same. The time between these two discoveries and Billy's hanging is so brief that Billy need not engage in the moral and psychological confusions that someone like Pierre goes through; before his end comes, Pierre is given great amounts of time for doubt, recoil, and the general spiritual withering that finally makes him unable to resist self-destruction. Billy does not have much chance for reflection, and so does not run the risk of losing or perverting his essential innocence. The meliorating effects of this compressed time scheme are only increased by the incident of Vere's visit. This is clear when Melville describes Billy's state of mind while chained on the upper gundeck just before his death.

> But now lying between the two guns, as nipped in the vice of fate, Billy's agony, mainly proceeding from a generous young heart's virgin experience of the diabolical incarnate and effective in some men—the tension of that agony was now over. It survived not the something healing in the closeted interview with Captain Vere. Without movement, he lay as in a trance, that adolescent expression previously noted as his taking on something akin to the look of a slumbering child in the cradle when the warm

hearth-glow of the still chamber at night plays on the dimples that at whiles mysteriously form in the cheek . . . . [P. 119]

Vere's "closeted interview" got Billy over what for all of Melville's orphans is the most critical stage of things—the first sighting of the world's duplicity and ambiguity. Vere's visit is not like Lucy's visit to the lonely Pierre in New York City, which only served to make deeper the darkness into which he had been heading. In *Billy Budd* the ministrations heal, not further wound. Melville, though he could not be false to his instinctive sense that innocence is not viable in this world, had also to be true to his belief that innocence can be capable of something more than moral confusion.

While *Billy Budd* was designed so that Billy could be rewarded, the work was also designed, as mentioned before, so that Vere could be vindicated. It must be admitted at the outset that Vere does suffer by comparison with Billy. Billy is innocent; when he strikes down Claggart, Vere even conceives of him as the avenging angel of God. And when he is hanged, he is portrayed by Melville as a crucified and transfigured Christ. In a situation as loaded as this, it can be difficult to see Vere as anything but a compromising, frightened weakling.[19] Melville, however, comes to grips with this difficulty quite early in the novel.

And here be it submitted that apparently going to corroborate the doctrine of man's Fall, a doctrine now popularly ignored, it is observable that where certain virtues pristine and unadulterate peculiarly characterize anybody in the external uniform of civilization, they will upon scrutiny seem not to be derived from custom or convention, but rather to be out of keeping with these, as if indeed exceptionally transmitted from a period prior to Cain's city and citified man. The character marked by such qualities has to an unvitiated taste an untampered-with flavor like that of berries, while the man thoroughly civilized,

> even in a fair specimen of the breed, has to the same
> moral palate a questionable smack as of a compounded
> wine. [Pp. 52-53]

As it turns out, Vere does emerge as a "fair specimen" of
civilized man; and though the passage's rhetoric is slippery, it
contains a warning to the reader about properly evaluating
someone like Vere. It admits that to a "moral palate" not
vitiated by "Cain's city," a person like Vere must inevitably
be less attractive than Billy. At the same time, even the "unvitiated taste" is still part of the period after man's Fall—the
period of "civilization." Therefore, it must live with compromise. It may respond more to Billy than to Vere, but Billy
is an unachievable ideal in this life. He is from another period
in time, another system. He can embody for the "citified
man" an act of faith in the final reward of innocence, but his
unvarying innocence is not a realizable, practical goal.

In fact, *Billy Budd* is ultimately Vere's novel. As Hayford
and Sealts' study of the growth of the manuscript shows,
Melville spent as much time and as many pages in revising
Vere's role in this story as he had on Billy's and Claggart's
roles combined.[20] Melville was not satisfied with the story as
it first existed in 1888, with Billy and Claggart as the main
characters and Vere only a minor one, because a narrative
focused only on the handsome sailor and the master-at-arms
would justify innocence but would not explore that vast mass
of humanity that had to struggle in the half-light of a post-
Adamic world. Melville was aware that in this world the
values Billy represents might, at times, have to be consciously
denied. Someone like Vere, then—the civilized captain who
has to make a choice between Billy and the civilization of
which he cannot avoid being part—becomes the natural vehi-
cle for dramatizing this idea.

Melville centers his portrayal of Vere on Vere's sense of
order and on the extent to which contingent circumstances
play a part in the decisions men must make. Vere staves off
chaos by being an uncompromising force for order. 'With

mankind,' he would say, 'forms, measured forms, are everything; and that is the import couched in the story of Orpheus with his lyre spellbinding the wild denizens of the wood' '' (p. 128). The arguments that are often brought to bear against an attitude like this are probably true, and Melville does not seek to deny them. First, the order that Vere holds onto, both in its military and legal aspects, is only a man-made one, and is used in the service of war. Also, it is an order that is capable of crushing someone like Billy, who is not disorderely, but rather has the habits of a peacemaker. In this light, Vere can seem orderly to the point of moral irresponsibility. To get a sense of just what Vere is committed to and why, however, one must go beyond any initial indignation and into Melville's sense of the structure of the postlapsarian world. One of the abiding conditions of man and his environment after the Fall is a fracture of harmony. Before the Fall, Adam and Eve lived in the Garden, and were at peace with themselves, the universe, and their God. Once driven out of the Garden, they and their descendants permanently lost all this. Therefore, if one believes in the perpetuation of anything positive, one has to at least try to create some substitute system of harmony to replace the one lost. Whatever this new order is, it can only hope to be partial, because of the very context of its creation. Only in art is complete harmony perhaps possible; but as Melville recognizes, art is not life, and "the symmetry of form attainable in pure fiction cannot so readily be achieved in a narration essentially having less to do with fable than with fact. Truth uncompromisingly told will always have its ragged edges . . ." (p. 128). An adherence to order, of course, was never enough for Melville. Captain Claret, aboard the Neversink, also kept the order of his ship, but in cruel and arbitrary ways. Vere, however, possesses humanity and common sense. He is never pompous or condescending. Melville shows that Vere, rather than belonging to that artificial sort of aristocracy White-Jacket encounters aboard the Neversink, possesses a greater and more basic kind of nobility, one proceeding "from a certain unaffected modesty of manhood sometimes accompanying a resolute nature." (p. 60). This is why, in the midst of the confusion and distrust after the spring uprisings, Vere's ship seems so peaceful. "In their general bearing and conduct the commissioned officers of a warship naturally take their tone from the commander, that is if he have that ascendancy of character that ought to be his" (p. 60). Vere's character is obviously ascendant.

It is true, Melville states, that Vere, "whatever his sterling qualities was without brilliant ones" (p. 61). He is not a Nelson; Melville considers Nelson a figure of truly exceptional force and brilliance, someone capable of ruling exclusively through the power of his own personality. Nelson was little concerned with anything like prudence, which, "even when dictated by quite other than selfish considerations, surely is no special virtue in a military man" (p. 58). Vere, on the hand, does make his decision in relation to Billy with one eye on the prudential (though not the selfish); and when he must enforce that decision on the crew, he has to resort to measured military forms (the muster and the drum) rather than the persuasive power of his personality alone. This, however, does not make Vere a pitiful weakling; it only makes him something less than Nelson. And as Melville treats Nelson, briefly, in the story, he is not so much a real person as he is what Richard Chase has called "a mythical hero standing behind Captain Vere."[21] He is a great and glorious master figure whose name is even more of a "trumpet to the blood" (p. 58) than is Wellington's. "Alfred in his funeral ode on [Wellington] ventures not to call him the greatest soldier of all time, though in the same ode he invokes Nelson as 'the greatest sailor since our world began' " (p. 58). "The [epic] poet but embodies in verse those exaltations of sentiment that a nature like Nelson, the opportunity being given, vitalizes into acts" (p. 58). Thus, to judge Vere by Nelson, just as to judge him by Billy, would be a mistake. Vere can only aspire to something less than Nelson or Billy. Nelson is kept mythically hovering in the background and Billy—"exceptionally transmitted from a period prior to Cain's city"—achieves his finest hour when he is transfigured at the masthead and achieves the stature also of a myth. Nelson and Billy are emblems of states that may inspire others to belief, but that are unattainable by almost everyone except themselves. Vere must try to keep steady on a somewhat lower level of perfection.

Vere, unfortunately, will only be able to hold out temporarily, because his world is too complex and dangerous. Melville builds this recognition into the form of the first five chapters. In chapters 1 and 2, he transfers Billy from the Rights of Man to the Bellipotent. Once this is accomplished, he devotes chapters 3 and 5 to a digression on the Nore and Spithead, using chapter 4 to introduce Nelson and a discussion of the increasingly mechanical, utilitarian nature of warfare since Nelson's time. In other words, in order to define the situation adequately that Billy and Vere will have to confront, Melville feels it necessary to go outside the limited context of the ship itself. If Melville's point of reference had remained inside the Bellipotent the conflict between Vere and Billy would have been relatively simple—Billy is right, Vere is wrong. Melville, however, deliberately sets the novel at a time when this kind of self-contained, straightforward struggle is not possible. Melville wants to digress because it is only through a digressive structure that he can dramatize his view of the post-lapsarian world—a world not only of fractured harmonies but of complex contingency, where it is impossible to limit an occurrence (whether historical, moral, or legal) within hard and fast boundaries. The form of the first five chapters, in effect, predicts the necessity of Billy's death and also the vindication of Vere's role in it. For Melville and Vere, both of whom are men who must live according to a less absolute scale of values than the one Billy represents, nothing can be easy, nothing is explainable without reference to other things.

Chapters 3 and 5 are especially interesting in this regard

because they show that it is impossible for Melville even to establish the *time* of the story's action without providing a history of the two mutinies and the legacy of fear they left behind them. The reason is that Melville does not deal in these chapters with clocks or calendars, but with periods of social and psychological time. The summer of 1797 is not an isolated moment or an isolated season. It is a coming together of influences from previous moments, which, in a larger and more real sense, determine *when* the story takes place. To talk only of clocks and calendars would be to be untrue to time as one actually experiences it, and so be unfair to the total meaning of people's actions.

If chapters 3 and 5 establish the complexity of a period like the summer of 1797, the digression of chapter 4, a view of the naval epoch of Vere and Nelson from a vantage point subsequent to that epoch, only helps to caution a reader further about too hastily judging the propriety of a historical action. Melville discusses the increasingly utilitarian nature of sea-warfare in his own day, with its reliance on technical innovation and efficiency rather than personal courage or decisiveness. In essence, technology seeks to reduce the human element in war as far as possible. This criticism of Melville's serves to create the sense that Nelson and Vere's epoch was a time when the burdens on the individual man, especially a commander, were larger and more personal than in Melville's century. Thus, while he centers the chapter on Nelson, Melville also demonstrates, by indirection, that the decisions of any officer (and so, someone like Vere) could not be easy ones during this period. They could not be decisions made with the detached efficiency of the "Benthamites of war" (p. 57) Melville sees as Nelson's successors. In this way, the chapter calls for a sympathetic appraisal of the Bellipotent's captain, a call reinforced by the warning Melville gives about too quickly judging certain of the actions of Nelson at Trafalgar: one should not criticize a commander on the basis of hindsight speculation about his conduct. "The *might-*

have-been is but boggy ground to build on" (p. 57), and the one thing no person can have is the capacity to look back on his own actions while he is in the process of performing them. Nor can one make choices on the basis of information one does not possess. So, a person cannot be judged by the hindsight of others, or by their seemingly superior information. What *"might-have-been"* becomes an almost impossible way of deciding the morality of an action. An individual can only be judged in the crucible of his own experience, in reference to those things he can know, and in reference to whether or not he responds to his knowledge with some semblance of humanity. " 'Forty years after a battle it is easy for a noncombatant to reason about how it ought to have been fought. It is another thing personally and under fire to have to direct the fighting while involved in the obscuring smoke of it . . .' " (p. 114).

Vere, while he is less frantic than many of his fellow captains, still cannot escape the pressure of his times. When Claggart comes to him with his alleged information about mutiny, he suggests that if Vere does not act on what is told him, the Bellipotent's fate may be that of a certain ship that obviously had trouble during the uprising at the Nore. Claggart is quite well aware that men live in the contexts created by circumstance, and he knows what kinds of emotional levers to work in order to get what he wants. His sense of this is flawless, for Vere's initial reaction shows that the Nore is a sore spot for him, though his outward demeanor aboard ship may not indicate it. He does not even give Claggart a chance to name the other ship.

> "Never mind that!" here peremptorily broke in [Vere], his face altering with anger, instinctively divining the ship that the other was about to name, one in which the Nore Mutiny had assumed a singularly tragical character that for a time jeopardized the life of its commander. Under the circumstances he was indignant at the proposed allusion. [P. 93]

To Vere's credit, however, he does not unnecessarily submit to the psychology of his time. His thoughts after this first flurried response testify not only to his shrewdness, but to his perception and presence of mind.

> But these thoughts and kindred dubious ones flitting across his mind were suddenly replaced by an intuitional surmise which, though as yet obscure in form, served practically to affect his reception of the ill tidings. Certain it is that, long versed in everything pertaining to the complicated gun-deck life, . . . Captain Vere did not permit himself to be unduly disturbed by the general tenor of his subordinate's report. [P. 93]

As a result, his decision is to conduct the affair as inconspicuously as possible. He wants a reasonable consideration of the matter.

Once Claggart is killed, of course, balance is upset; or, more properly, Vere is called upon to perform a more complicated act of balance than he anticipated. He must now consider the problem of absolute as opposed to human justice, and of his personal regard for Billy as opposed to his sense of duty. He thus becomes more agitated in his behavior. Whether one should be led by this new agitation of Vere's to doubt his sanity, as the ship's surgeon does, is a very debatable point, however. In fact, the whole sanity issue, as Melville presents it, is so much one of speculation, degees, and suppositions, that it is really not an issue at all.

> Who in the rainbow can draw the line where the violet tint ends and the orange tint begins? Distinctly we see the difference of the colors, but where exactly does the one first blendingly enter into the other? So with sanity and insanity. In pronounced cases there is no question about them. But in some supposed cases, in various degrees supposedly less pronounced, to draw the exact line of demarcation few will undertake, though for a fee becoming considerate some professional experts will. There is nothing namable but that some men will, or undertake to, do it for pay. [P. 102]

This is the deliberately obscuring prose of *The Confidence-Man*. By the time the passage is over, the question has evaporated, as Melville intended it to. However, what for Melville are not suppositions, but facts, are the circumstances of Vere's actions.

> That the unhappy event which has been narrated could not have happened at a worse juncture was but too true . . . . Moreover, there was something crucial in the case.
> . . . .
> Small wonder then that the Bellipotent's captain, though in general a man of rapid decision, felt that circumspectness not less than promptitude was necessary. [Pp. 102-103]

Interestingly enough, the tone and direction of these passages in which Melville speaks resemble those of Vere in his opening statement to the drumhead court.

> "... I ... perceive in you— ... a troubled hesitancy, proceeding, I doubt not, from the clash of military duty with moral scruple—scruple vitalized by compassion. For the compassion, how can I otherwise than share it? But, mindful of paramount obligations, I strive against scruples that may tend to enervate decision. Not, gentlemen, that I hide from myself that the case is an exceptional one. Speculatively regarded, it might well be referred to a jury of casuists. But for us here, acting not as casuists or moralists, it is a case practical, and under martial law practically to be dealt with." [P. 110]

Vere argues that while there are areas of the Budd case that could be debated endlessly (as critics have), there are still certain facts of circumstance that take precedence and make the situation nothing more or less than what it must be. Therefore, Melville himself was preparing the reader to accept Vere's view when he followed his very ambiguous treatment of sanity with the statement that, in calling the drumhead court, Vere did only what the conjoined forces of the moment made it necessary for him to do. This leads the reader away from polar abstractions like "sanity" and "insanity," "justice" and "injustice," and toward a sense of necessity in human conduct, precisely the direction in which Vere is trying to lead the court. Melville, of course, is not affirming that man's actions should be amoral; nor is Vere. Author and character alike are sensitive to the moral ambiguity involved in condemning Billy to death. But human actions always take place in a context of circumstances, which context often makes abstract questions not only unanswerable, but largely irrelevant.

The case that Vere presents to the court, therefore, embodies his own circumstantial view of the world. It is not calculated to win a more liberal reader's sympathy (nor does it truly win the support of his own officers). The source of his case lies in his need uncompromisingly, but in good faith, to "demonstrate certain principles that were axioms to himself" (p. 109). He must tell what to him is the truth. Not the whole truth—he admits that his arguments do not encompass absolute, divine justice, and that they ask for his officers to suspend their normal sense of freedom and compassion. What Vere feels required to tell is that portion of the total truth that can have meaning for a ship at sea, at war, and subject to the Mutiny Act at a time just after the Nore. And if one looks at the arguments he presents, there is a consistent, justifiable logic to them.

First of all, there is Vere's reliance on the deed of murder itself, rather than the intent. This may distress a reader, as it does the court. But if Vere were to hold Billy over for trial by the Admiralty, they, too, would have to rely on Billy's deed; for, as Melville comments, "in the light of that martial code whereby it was formally to be judged, innocence and guilt personified in Claggart and Budd in effect changed places" (p. 103). Melville admits that "the essential right and wrong involved in the matter, the clearer that might be, so much the worse for the responsibility of a loyal sea commander, inasmuch as he was not authorized to determine the matter on that primitive basis" (p. 103). This code will not miraculously alter itself between the Bellipotent and the Admiralty; if anything, the Admiralty will have an even greater sense of loyalty and responsibility toward naval law than the individual commander.

The second principal argument of Vere's, which again might rub one's abstract moral sensibilities the wrong way, is the assertion that by their very condition as sailors, Vere and his officers owe their allegiance to the king rather than Nature, and that "in receiving our commissions we in the most important regards ceased to be natural free agents" (p. 110). All through his writings, however, Melville made it clear that no one is a free agent. A person is always ultimately a slave: to his destiny (like Israel Potter), to his own personality and compulsions (like Taji or Ahab), to his own final ignorance (like Ishmael), or to the tradition in which he finds himself (like Pierre). All of Melville's protagonists are slaves in one way or another; and their attempts to sever whatever bonds confine them and return to some state of natural free agency lead either to destruction or anticlimax. The kind of assumption that seems to underlie Vere's statements on freedom, therefore, is not at variance with what Melville had always believed. If ultimate freedom is a false pursuit, a person must choose a lesser species of freedom. Hopefully, it will be one which, like Vere's, can contribute to some sense of order and harmony, and not one like the French Revolution, which initially promised a new and greater liberty, but which, in attempting to fulfill that promise, inevitably became a force for disorder and destruction.

Vere's putting aside his allegiance to Nature may also stem from a very special confrontation he has had with Nature all through his naval life. Just before delivering his address to the court, Vere looks out at the ocean, something he will do from time to time. He calls the ocean "inviolate Nature primeval" (p. 110), but what he finds there is the "monotonous blank of the twilight sea" (p. 109). That is what he always finds. Thus, appeals to Nature serve little purpose for him. It, like God, is silent. This was the lesson embodied in Ishmael's confrontation with the great whale in *Moby-Dick*—ultimately, one must perform all one's actions in ignorance. Vere can only seek survival for his men and himself within the limits that his human ignorance imposes. He must resist chaos without the final knowledge of the direction in which his resistance will take him.

While the arguments that Vere advances are attempts to define man's limited position in a post-Edenic environment, his officers, on the other hand, would prefer to oppose this sense of limitation by keeping Billy alive. Billy becomes for Vere's officers what Milton Stern calls a "lure,"[22] something that leads men to try to pass beyond the fixed boundaries of their nature and so become questers after some ideal condition of life (Typee Valley, Yillah, and Redburn's guidebook are all lures). Billy is the prelapsarian innocent who appears suddenly among the men of "Cain's city," and these men seek to perpetuate what Billy represents by foregoing the system that has been responsible for preserving some small order in their essentially disharmonious world. Vere is the only one who holds out against the absorptive power of the lure, the only one who realizes that "given the . . . actuality of earth and time, then the transcendent purity, the Edenic, absolute morality, is something before history and which therefore comes from nowhere—is something that is literally as impossible as Yillah . . . or Billy himself."[23] Vere even disallows his officers' suggestion that they convict Billy but mitigate the punishment. His argument is that the men aboard ship would have no frame of reference for evaluating that rather ambiguous legal action, and so it would do more harm than good. If one recalls what happened to Pierre—a character who did not possess the ability to evaluate ambiguity—it is easier to appreciate what Vere wants to prevent.

Through all of this, Vere is not an irresponsible authoritarian. It is true that no one on the court, because of

Vere's position, could oppose his arguments seriously, no matter what arguments he advanced. It is also true that he uses his office to bring about a decision that he feels is essential, regardless of what others feel; he does not confine himself simply to the role of witness. Still, he knows it is necessary to show why a particular kind of choice must be made. Men cannot survive without knowledge, and Vere's role is that of an instructor in reality to those around him who would encourage unrealistic attitudes.

Vere is, of course, attracted to Billy in the same way his officers are, perhaps even more intensely. This is evident in the history of his personal relationship with Billy. Vere has a weakness that Melville touches on in the early chapters—his aloofness. In those moods that accompany Vere's gazing out to sea, he realizes the individual's essential loneliness and ignorance; and so, while he performs his duties well, and is sensitive to the needs of his men, he never really gets close to anyone. When Billy arrives aboard the Bellipotent, and Vere is suddenly face to face with almost total innocence, he, like his men, is drawn to the handsome sailor's other-worldliness: Billy is incapable of reflection and so ignorant of all those unpleasant things Vere has come to understand as axiomatic. In addition to this, and because of it, Billy is uniquely personable. Vere, therefore, arranges for Billy to work near him; he plans on promoting him; in the interview with Billy and Claggart, he shows Billy the greatest kindness; he wants to see Billy cleared of the allegations against him. At the same time, however, Vere's desire to protect Billy is based on knowledge, not sentimental idealism. Vere seems all along to have recognized that there is something fatal to Billy in the structure of the world. This is why, when Billy kills Claggart, when he violates the law and so ceases to be outside or above it, Vere immediately calls him "Fated boy" (p. 99). Vere is not prejudging Billy, or looking for a way to get rid of him and the problem he presents. He is simply stating what he knows to be inevitably true and axiomatic. Vere had tried to sustain Billy outside the lines of force created by those axioms; but when Billy violates his own immunity, the rest follows automatically.

Nor does Vere's prosecution of Billy imply any reduction in his humane sympathy for the sailor. It only means that his sympathy must be put in a new context—one, in fact, more personally difficult for Vere. Vere still feels a need to protect Billy, at least as far as circumstances allow. And so, he acts to reconcile Billy to his fate by creating for him a sense of death that will not be prey to bitterness or misanthropy. He need not make his final visit to Billy; it is not part of his official role in the proceedings. What it costs him emotionally is displayed in his face as he leaves the compartment in which Billy is being kept.

> The first to encounter Captain Vere in act of leaving the compartment was the senior lieutenant. The face he beheld, for the moment one expressive of the agony of the strong, was to that officer, though a man of fifty, a startling revelation . . . . [T]he condemned one suffered less than he who mainly had effected the condemnation . . . . [P. 115]

Vere will pay this emotional price because, while opting for a system of regulated life, Vere can never simply be a military functionary—dead, orderly, without compassion or love. This is why, when Vere visits Billy, Melville establishes an essential identity between them. Both share "radically . . . in the rarer qualities of our nature" (pp. 114-115). Whatever took place in that compartment, Melville describes it as a "sacrament" (p. 115). Billy, the filial innocent, is reconciled to his betrayer, "the leader who recognizes that the historical moment demands the sacrifice of self to the possible victory that the combined head and heart may achieve."[24] The middle ground, when it is inhabited by someone like Vere, can become a place of honor, a place of importance, and not just an area for weak-willed expediency.

Thus, regardless of Vere's limitations, what Melville respects in him is the very pattern of dutiful masculine conduct Melville had never been able to conform himself to in any conclusive way. And perhaps right up until his death Melville never did completely want to conform himself to that pattern, regardless of how much he could accept Vere's behavior as the only sensible course for a man to take. One indication of this continued resistance is the very oblique quality of *Billy Budd*. Rarely does Melville directly state his feelings about Vere; usually he comes at them by indirection and subtle juxtaposition. Part of Melville, finally, hangs back from giving open sanction to Vere; he is too much a man of realities for even an aging and resigned Melville. But more revealing, perhaps, is the piece of paper, pasted out of sight at Melville's writing desk, which read, "Keep true to the dreams of thy youth."[25] Curious that it would be out of sight, a reflection of Melville's knowledge that the dreams of youth are too simple, too uncomplicated to be guides for "grown-up" living. But the motto was kept by Melville's side as he wrote because it expressed, truly, the thing that he wanted. "If we but knew what these dreams were!" says Eleanor Metcalf. "That they grew out of the deepest needs of the whole man seems certain. That they reflected a desire to nourish the roots of life, I believe."[26] But one might have cause to disagree with Mrs. Metcalf that the dreams "were religious in nature."[27] They were probably much simpler than that. They were probably dreams of calm sunlight in a comfortable room as one waits for the daily return of the man who seems always to fill the room with substance; and dreams of ships that sail perpetually through clear weather, with captains strong, and true, and loving. They were, in fact, dreams of fathers, chieftains of their races and climes whose arms never wearied, and whose wills never faltered. In everything else (that is, in reality) there was only finally the deathlike touch of wet sea stones, the ominous vapor of the haglet's breath, and the knife-edged fin of the shark.

The year before Herman's birth, Allan Melville wrote to his wife from Liverpool, "[T]each our tender Babes as far as their little hearts are susceptible of impressions to cherish the recollections of their absent Father."[28] Though Herman was not yet around, it seems to be he, of all the Melville children, who turned out to be the most "susceptible of impressions" of an absent Allan Melville. Herman, the lost boy (he would have sympathized with Thomas Wolfe) died in 1891, having never found again the security he had long ago lost, and leaving behind him work after work that chronicled an incomplete life, a life with no harbor gained because the final harbor was only a dream over sixty years old.

Notes

1. Letter to Hawthorne, 17 November 1851, in Merrell R. Davis and William H. Gilman, eds., *The Letters of Herman Melville* (New Haven: Yale University Press, 1960), p. 143.

2. Ibid., p. 142.

3. Ibid.

4. Letter to Sophia Hawthorne, 8 January 1852, ibid., p. 146.

5. Eleanor Melville Metcalf, *Herman Melville: Cycle and Epicycle* (Cambridge: Harvard University Press, 1953), p. 133.

6. Harrison Hayford, Hershel Parker, and G. Thomas Tanselle, eds., *Pierre* (Evanston and Chicago: Northwestern University Press and the Newberry Library, 1971).

7. William Ellery Sedgwick, *Herman Melville: the Tragedy of Mind* (New York: Russell and Russell, 1962), p. 157.

8. Milton Stern, *The Fine Hammered Steel of Herman Melville* (Urbana: University of Illinois Press, 1957), pp. 162-163.

9. See letters to Hawthorne between 25 July 1852 and late November of the same year, in Davis and Gilman, pp. 152-163.

10. Leon Howard, *Herman Melville* (Berkeley: University of California Press, 1951), p. 217.

11. Ibid., p. 208.

12. John Seelye, *Melville: The Ironic Diagram* (Evanston: Northwestern University Press, 1970), p. 112.

13. Warner Berthoff, ed., *Great Short Works of Herman Melville* (New York: Harper and Row, 1970), p. 110.

14. Henry A. Murray, introduction to the Hendricks House edition of *Pierre* (New York: Hendricks House, Farrar, Straus, 1949), p. xv.

15. Thomas H. Johnson, ed., "A narrow Fellow in the Grass," #986 in *Final Harvest: Emily Dickinson's Poems* (Boston: Little, Brown and Co., 1961), p. 229.

16. Seelye, p. 76.

17. Edgar A. Dryden, *Melville's Thematics of Form* (Baltimore: Johns Hopkins Press, 1968), p. 199.

18. Harrison Hayford and Merton M. Sealts, Jr., eds., *Billy Budd, Sailor* (Chicago: University of Chicago Press, 1962).

19. One of the most articulate statements of this perspective is still Merlin Bowen's in *The Long Encounter* (Chicago: University of Chicago Press, 1960), pp. 216-233.

20. Hayford and Sealts, in their preface to *Billy Budd,* p. 2.

21. Richard Chase, *Herman Melville: A Critical Study* (New York: The Macmillan Company, 1949), p. 275.

22. Stern, pp. 15-16.

23. Ibid., p. 212.

24. Ibid., p. 208.

25. Metcalf, p. 284.

26. Ibid.

27. Ibid.

28. William H. Gilman, *Melville's Early Life and Redburn* (New York: New York University Press, 1951), p. 13.

Bibliography

Anderson, Charles R. "Contemporary American Opinions of *Typee* and *Omoo*," *American Literature* 9 (1937):1-25.

———.*Melville in the South Seas.* New York: Columbia University Press, 1939.

Arvin, Newton. *Herman Melville.* New York: William Sloane Associates, 1950.

Aubin, Robert Arnold. *Topographical Poetry in XVIII-Century England.* New York: The Modern Language Association of America, 1936.

Baird, James R. *Ishmael.* Baltimore, Md.: Johns Hopkins Press, 1956.

———."The Noble Polynesian," *The Pacific Spectator* 4 (1950): 452-465.

Beatty, Lillian. "Typee and Blithedale: Rejected Ideal Communities," *Personalist* 37 (1956):367-378.

Bercovitch, Sacvan. "Melville's Search for National Identity: Son and Father in *Redburn, Pierre,* and *Billy Budd*," *College Language Association Journal* 10 (1967): 217-228.

Berthoff, Warner. *The Example of Melville.* Princeton, N.J.: Princeton University Press, 1962.

Bowen, Merlin. *The Long Encounter.* Chicago: University of Chicago Press, 1960.

———."*Redburn* and the Angle of Vision," *Modern Philology* 52 (1954): 100-109.

Brashers, H.C. "Ishmael's Tattoos," *Sewanee Review* 70 (1962): 137-154.

Braswell, William. *Melville's Religious Thought.* New York: Pageant Books, 1959.

Bredahl, A. Carl. *Melville's Angles of Vision.* Gainesville, Fla.: University of Florida Press, 1972.

Brodtkorb, Paul. *Ishmael's White World.* New Haven, Conn.: Yale University Press, 1965.

Browne, Ray B. *Melville's Drive to Humanism.* Lafayette, Ind.: Purdue University Studies, 1971.

Chase, Richard P. *Herman Melville.* New York: The Macmillan Company, 1949.

Cambon, Glauco. "Ishmael and the Problem of Formal Discontinuities in *Moby-Dick,*" *Modern Language Notes* 76 (1961): 516-523.

Carothers, Robert Lee. *Melville and the Search for the Father.* Unpublished doctoral dissertation, Kent State University, 1969.

Crews, Frederick C. *The Sins of the Fathers.* New York: Oxford University Press, 1966.

Davis, Merrell R. "The Flower Symbolism in *Mardi,*" *Modern Language Quarterly* 2 (1941): 626-638.

———.*Melville's Mardi: A Chartless Voyage.* New Haven, Conn.: Yale University Press, 1952.

Dickinson, Emily. *Final Harvest: Emily Dickinson's Poems.* Ed. Thomas H. Johnson. Boston: Little, Brown, and Co., 1961.

Dillingham, William B. *An Artist in the Rigging: the Early Work of Herman Melville.* Athens, Georgia: University of Georgia Press, 1972.

Dryden, Edgar A. *Melville's Thematics of Form.* Baltimore, Md.: Johns Hopkins Press, 1968.

Emerson, Ralph Waldo. *Selections from Ralph Waldo Emerson.* Ed. Stephen E. Whicher. Boston: Houghton, Mifflin Co., 1957.

Finkelstein, Dorothee Metlitsky. *Melville's Orienda.* New Haven, Conn.: Yale University Press, 1961.

Firebaugh, Joseph J. "Humorist as Rebel: The Melville of *Typee,*" *Nineteenth Century Fiction* 9 (1954): 108-121.

Fogle, Richard Harter. *Melville's Shorter Tales.* Norman, Oklahoma: University of Oklahoma Press, 1960.

Forrey, Robert. "Herman Melville and the Negro Question," *Mainstream* 15, 2 (1962): 23-32.

Franklin, H. Bruce. "Redburn's Wicked End," *Nineteenth Century Fiction* 20 (1965): 190-194.

————.*The Wake of the Gods.* Stanford, Cal.: Stanford University Press, 1963.

Gilman, William H. *Melville's Early Life and Redburn.* New York: New York University Press, 1951.

Gleim, William S. *The Meaning of Moby-Dick.* New York: Russell and Russell, 1938.

Gohdes, Clarence. "Melville's Friend 'Toby'," *Modern Language Notes* 59 (1944):52-55.

Grejda, Edward. *The Common Continent of Men: Racial Equality in the Writings of Herman Melville.* Port Washington, N.Y.: Kennikat Press, 1974.

⚹ Haberstroh, Charles J. *"Redburn:* the Psychological Pattern," *Studies in American Fiction* 2, 2 (1974):133-145.

⚹ ————."Melville, Marriage, and *Mardi,"* *Studies in the Novel* 9 (1977):247-261.

Hall, James B. *"Moby-Dick:* Parable of a Dying System," *Western Review* 14 (1950):223-226.

Heimert, Alan. *"Moby-Dick* and American Political Symbolism," *American Quarterly* 15 (1963): 498-534.

Hetherington, Hugh W. *Melville's Reviewers, British and American, 1846-1891.* Chapel Hill, N.C.: University of North Carolina Press, 1961.

Hillway, Tyrus. *Herman Melville.* New York: Twayne Publishers, Inc., 1963.

————."Taji's Abdication in Herman Melville's *Mardi,"* *American Literature* 16 (1944): 204-207.

————."Taji's Quest for Certainty," *American Literature* 18 (1946): 27-34.

Hillway, Tyrus, and Mansfield, Luther S., eds. *Moby-Dick Centennial Essays.* Dallas, Texas: Southern Methodist University Press, 1953.

Hirsch, David H. "The Dilemma of the Liberal Intellectual: Melville's Ishmael," *Texas Studies in Literature and Language*

5 (1963):169-188.

Hoeltje, Hubert H. "Hawthorne, Melville, and 'Blackness'," *American Literature* 37 (1965): 41-51.

Hoffman, Daniel G. *Form and Fable in American Literature.* New York: Oxford University Press, 1961.

Houghton, Donald E. "The Incredible Ending of Melville's *Typee,*" *Emerson Society Quarterly* 22 (1961):28-31.

Howard, Leon. *Herman Melville.* Berkeley and Los Angeles, Cal.: University of California Press, 1951.

Kaplan, Sidney. "Herman Melville and the Whaling Enderbys," *American Literature* 24 (1952): 224-229.

Kenney, Alice P. *The Gansevoorts of Albany.* Syracuse, N.Y.: Syracuse University Press, 1969.

Kenny, Vincent. *Herman Melville's Clarel.* Hamden, Conn.: Archon Books, 1973.

Kosok, Heinz. "Redburn's Image of Childhood," *Emerson Society Quarterly* 39 (1965):40-42.

Lawrence, D. H. *Studies in Classic American Literature.* New York: Doubleday and Co., Inc., 1951.

Lebowitz, Alan. *Progress Into Silence.* Bloomington, Ind.: Indiana University Press, 1970.

Leiter, Louis. "Queequeg's Coffin," *Nineteenth Century Fiction* 13 (December, 1958): 249-254.

Levin, Harry. *The Power of Blackness.* New York: Alfred A. Knopf, Inc., 1958.

Lewis, R. W. B. *The American Adam.* Chicago: University of Chicago Press, 1955.

Leyda, Jay, ed. *The Melville Log.* 2 vols. New York: Harcourt, Brace, and Co., 1951.

Marx, Leo. *The Machine in the Garden.* New York: Oxford University Press, 1964.

Mason, Ronald. *The Spirit Above the Dust.* London: John Lehmann, 1951.

Mathiessen, F. O. *American Renaissance.* New York: Oxford University Press, 1941.

Maxwell, D. E. S. *Herman Melville.* London: Routledge and Kegan Paul, 1968.

Melville, Herman. *The Battle Pieces of Herman Melville*. Ed. Hennig Cohen. New York: Thomas Yoseloff, 1963.

———.*Billy Budd, Sailor*. Ed. Harrison Hayford and Merton M. Sealts, Jr. Chicago: University of Chicago Press, 1962.

———.*Clarel*. Ed. Walter Bezanson. New York: Hendricks House, Inc., 1960.

———.*Collected Poems*. Ed. Howard P. Vincent. Chicago: Packard and Co., 1947.

———.*The Confidence-Man*. Ed. H. Bruce Franklin. Indianapolis, Ind.: The Bobbs-Merrill Company, Inc., 1967.

———.*Great Short Works of Herman Melville*. Ed. Warner Berthoff. New York: Harper and Row Publishers, Inc., 1970.

———.*Israel Potter*. New York: G. P. Putnam and Co., 1855.

———.*John Marr and Other Sailors*. New York: The DeVinne Press, 1888.

———.*Journal Up the Straits*. Ed. Raymond Weaver. New York: Cooper Square Publishers, Inc., 1971.

———.*Journal of a Visit to Europe and the Levant*. Ed. Howard C. Horsford. Princeton, N.J.: Princeton University Press, 1955.

———.*Journal of a Visit to London and the Continent*. Ed. Eleanor Melville Metcalf. Cambridge, Mass.: Harvard University Press, 1948.

———.*The Letters of Herman Melville*. Ed. Merrell R. Davis and William H. Gilman. New Haven, Conn.: Yale University Press, 1960.

———.*Mardi*. Ed. Harrison Hayford, Hershel Parker, and G. Thomas Tanselle. Evanston and Chicago: Northwestern University Press and the Newberry Library, 1970.

———.*Moby-Dick*. Ed. Harrison Hayford and Hershel Parker. New York: W. W. Norton and Company, Inc., 1967.

———.*Omoo*. Ed. Harrison Hayford, Hershel Parker, and G. Thomas Tanselle. Evanston and Chicago: Northwestern University Press and the Newberry Library, 1968.

———.*Pierre*. Ed. Harrison Hayford, Hershel Parker, and G. Thomas Tanselle. Evanston and Chicago: Northwestern University Press and the Newberry Library, 1971.

———.*Pierre*. Ed. Henry A. Murray. New York: Hendricks

House, Farrar, Straus, 1949.

————.*Redburn*. Ed. Harrison Hayford, Hershel Parker, and G. Thomas Tanselle. Evanston and Chicago: Northwestern University Press and the Newberry Library, 1969.

————.*Timoleon*. New York: The Caxton Press, 1891.

————.*Typee*. Ed. Harrison Hayford, Hershel Parker, and G. Thomas Tanselle. Evanston and Chicago: Northwestern University Press and the Newberry Library, 1968.

————.*White-Jacket*. Ed. Harrison Hayford, Hershel Parker, and G. Thomas Tanselle. Evanston and Chicago: Northwestern University Press and the Newberry Library, 1970.

Metcalf, Eleanor Melville. *Herman Melville: Cycle and Epicycle*. Cambridge, Mass.: Harvard University Press, 1953.

Miller, Edwin Haviland. *Melville*. New York: George Braziller, Inc., 1975.

Miller, James E. *A Reader's Guide to Herman Melville*. New York: Farrar, Straus, and Cudahy, 1962.

————.*"Redburn* and *White-Jacket:* Initiation and Baptism," *Nineteenth Century Fiction* 13 (1959): 273-293.

Moore, Maxine. *That Lonely Game: Melville, Mardi, and the Almanac*. Columbia, Missouri: University of Missouri Press, 1975.

Mumford, Lewis. *Herman Melville*. New York: The Literary Guild of America, 1929.

Olson, Charles. *Call Me Ishmael*. New York: Reynal and Hitchcock, 1947.

Percival, M. O. *A Reading of Moby-Dick*. Chicago: University of Chicago Press, 1950.

The Picture of Liverpool. Liverpool, 1808.

Pommer, Henry F. *Milton and Melville*. Pittsburgh, Pa: University of Pittsburgh Press, 1950.

Rampersad, Arnold. *Melville's Israel Potter*. Bowling Green, Ohio: Bowling Green University Popular Press, 1969.

Rosenberry, Edward H. *Melville and the Comic Spirit*. Cambridge, Mass.: Harvard University Press, 1955.

Schroeter, James. *"Redburn* and the Failure of Mythic Criticism," *American Literature* 39 (1967): 279-297.

Sealts, Merton M. *The Early Lives of Melville.* Madison, Wisconsin: University of Wisconsin Press, 1974.

Sedgwick, William Ellery, *Herman Melville: The Tragedy of Mind.* New York: Russell and Russell, 1962.

Seelye, John. *Melville: The Ironic Diagram.* Evanston, Ill.: Northwestern University Press, 1970.

———."The Structure of Encounter: Melville's Review of Hawthorne's *Mosses,*" rpt. in *Melville and Hawthorne in the Berkshires: A Symposium.* Ed. Howard P. Vincent. Kent, Ohio: Kent State University Press, 1968, pp. 63-69.

Shurr, William H. *The Mystery of Iniquity: Melville as Poet, 1857-1891.* Lexington, Ky.: University Press of Kentucky, 1972.

Slochower, Harry. *"Moby-Dick:* The Myth of Democratic Expectancy," *American Quarterly* 2 (1950): 259-269.

Stafford William T. *Melville's Billy Budd and the Critics.* Belmont, Cal.: Wadsworth Publishing Co., 1968.

Stanton, Robert. *"Typee* and Milton: Paradise Well Lost," *Modern Language Notes* 74 (1959): 407-411.

Stephens, Leslie and Lee, Sidney, eds. *Dictionary of National Biography.* 22 vols. London: Oxford University Press, 1937-1938, 1: 186; 17: 222-225.

Stern, Milton R. *The Fine Hammered Steel of Herman Melville.* Urbana, Ill.: University of Illinois Press, 1957.

Stone, Geoffrey. *Melville.* New York: Sheed and Ward, 1949.

The Stranger in Liverpool. Liverpool, 1816.

Tabachnik, Norman. "Creative Suicidal Crises," *Archives of General Psychiatry* 29 (1973): 258-263.

Thompson, Lawrance. *Melville's Quarrel with God.* Princeton, N.J.: Princeton University Press, 1952.

Thorp, Willard. *Herman Melville: Representative Selections.* New York: American Book Co., 1938.

———."Redburn's Prosy Old Guidebook," *PMLA* 53 (1938): 1146-1156.

*Travis, Mildred K. *"Mardi:* Melville's Allegory of Love," *Emerson Society Quarterly* 43 (1966): 88-94.

Van Cromphout, Gustaaf. "Herman Melville's *Redburn* Considered in the Light of the Elder Henry James's *The Nature of Evil,*" *Revue des Langues Vivantes* 29 (1963): 117-126.

Vincent, Howard P. *The Tailoring of Melville's White-Jacket.* Evanston, Ill.: Northwestern University Press, 1970.

―――. *The Trying-Out of Moby-Dick.* Boston: Houghton, Mifflin Co., 1949.

―――,ed. *Twentieth Century Interpretations of Billy Budd.* Englewood Cliffs, N.J.: Prentice-Hall, Inc., 1971.

―――."*White-Jacket:* An Essay in Interpretation," *New England Quarterly,* 22 (1949): 304-315.

Weathers, Willie T. "*Moby-Dick* and the Nineteenth-Century Scene," *Texas Studies in Literature and Language* 1 (1960): 477-501.

Weaver, Raymond N. *Herman Melville, Mariner and Mystic.* New York: Pageant Books, 1961.

Weissbuck, Ted N., and Stillians, Bruce. "Ishmael the Ironist: The Anti-Salvation Theme in *Moby-Dick,*" *Emerson Society Quarterly* 31 (1963): 71-75.

Widmer, Kingsley. *The Ways of Nihilism: A Study of Herman Melville's Short Novels.* Los Angeles, Cal.: California State Colleges, 1970.

Wright, Nathalia. *Melville's Use of the Bible.* Durham, N.C.: Duke University Press, 1949.

―――."The Head and Heart in Melville's *Mardi,*" *PMLA* 66 (1951): 351-362.

Zoellner, Robert. *The Salt-Sea Mastodon: a Reading of Moby-Dick.* Berkeley, Cal.: University of California Press, 1973.

Index